T0043449

The Poems of Sidney West

JUAN GELMAN (Buenos Aires, Argentina, 1930) is one of the most read and influential poets in the Spanish language. He has published more than twenty books of poetry since 1956 and has been translated into fourteen languages. A political activist and critical journalist since his youth, Gelman has not only been a literary paradigm but also a moral one, within and outside of Argentina. Among his most recent awards are the National Poetry Prize (Argentina, 1997), the Juan Rulfo Prize in Latin American and Caribbean Literature (Mexico, 2000), the Pablo Neruda Prize (Chile, 2005), the Queen Sofia Prize in Ibero-American Poetry (Spain, 2005), and the Cervantes Prize (the most important award given to a Hispanic writer, Spain, 2007).

Earthworks Series

Series Editors: Katherine Hedeen, Gordon Henry Jr,
Janet McAdams & Víctor Rodríguez Núñez

The Poems of Sidney West
Los poemas de Sidney West

JUAN GELMAN

English versions by
KATHERINE HEDEEN
& VÍCTOR RODRÍGUEZ NÚÑEZ

SALT

CAMBRIDGE

PUBLISHED BY SALT PUBLISHING
14a High Street, Fulbourn, Cambridge CB21 5DH United Kingdom

First Edition: Editorial Galerna, Buenos Aires, 1969

Salt Publishing 2008

Printed and bound in the United States by Lightning Source Inc

Typeset in Swift 9.5 / 13

ISBN 978 1 84471 464 3 paperback

Salt Publishing Ltd gratefully acknowledges
the financial assistance of Arts Council England

1 3 5 7 9 8 6 4 2

Contents

Acknowledgements

The translators wish to gratefully acknowledge the National Endowment for the Arts (USA) for its support of this project and the poet Juan Gelman for his unwavering encouragement and collaboration.

Juan Gelman: Translation as Fidelity

This edition offers at last the splendid poems of Sidney West to English readers, supposedly their original addressees. West is among the best imaginary poets not only of Whitman's native land, allegedly his as well, but of all possible lands. His texts, although rich with exceptional life experience, will satisfy those who still believe in "the death of the author." No less satisfied, in spite of his anti-romanticism, will be those captivated by "committed writing." And in another paradox that West himself would have loved, if he had existed, what's offered here constitutes a translation of a translation. In other words, an English version based on the prior version into Spanish apparently completed in 1969 by the notable Argentine poet Juan Gelman (Buenos Aires, 1930). He and only he, until the contrary is proven, should be considered the authentic, industrious author of the author of these poems, and the poems themselves.

Juan Gelman is the most significant, contemporary Argentine intellectual figure and one of the most read and influential poets in the Spanish language. Son of a family of Jewish immigrants from the Ukraine, he grew up like any other *porteño*, among soccer and tango, in the populous neighborhood of Villa Crespo. He was initiated into reading by his brother Boris, who would often recite Pushkin's verses to him in Russian. He also received from Boris the works of Hugo, Dostoyevsky, Tolstoy, and other modern and contemporary classics. At 11, he published his first poem in the magazine *Rojo y negro*, and in the 1950s formed part of the group of rebel writers, *El Pan Duro*. He was discovered by Raúl González Túñón, among the most relevant voices of the southern country's poetic avant-garde, who saw in the young man's verses "a rich and vivacious lyricism and a principally social content [...] that does not elude the richness of fantasy."[1]

Juan Gelman has published, from his initial *Violín y otras cuestiones* (1956) to his most recent *Mundar* (2008), more than twenty books of poetry.[2] These works, as Mario Benedetti asserted early on, constitute "the most coherent, and also the most daring, participatory repertoire (in spite of its inevitable wells of solitude), and ultimately the one most suited to its environment, that Argentine poetry has today."[3] We would add Hispanic poetry in general, as the profusion of re-editions of his books and numerous anthologies proves.[4] Gelman's poetry has achieved international recognition, with translations into more than ten languages, including English.[5] Among his most recent awards are the National Poetry Prize (Argentina, 1997), the Juan Rulfo Prize in Latin American and Caribbean Literature (Mexico, 2000), the Pablo Neruda Prize (Chile, 2005), the Queen Sofia Prize in Ibero-American Poetry (Spain, 2005), and the Cervantes Prize (Spain, 2007). No one should be surprised to see him the winner of the Nobel Prize in Literature one day.

In this retelling, it would be as well to note that Juan Gelman has not only been a literary paradigm but also a moral one, within and outside of Argentina. Political activist and critical journalist since his youth, he was forced into an exile of thirteen years because of the military dictatorship that ravaged his country from 1976 to 1983, and the weak governments that immediately followed. In 1976 the ultra-right kidnapped his children, Nora Eva, 19, and Marcelo Ariel, 20, along with his son's wife, María Claudia Iruretagoyena, 19, who was 7 months pregnant. Nora Eva would later return, unlike his son and daughter-in-law, who were killed; their child born in a concentration camp. The vehement search for the truth about the fate of these family members, which culminated in finding his granddaughter in Uruguay in 2000, has made the poet a symbol of the struggle for respect for human rights.

Like other poets from his time and space, Juan Gelman creates his work starting from a critique of the so-called post-avant-garde poetry, which surges in the Hispanic world in the 1940s and breaks with the powerful avante-garde. A poet who denies the labors of the Mexican Octavio Paz, the Cuban José Lezama Lima, the Argentine Alberto Girri, among others, to reaffirm it in his own way. As Benedetti has pointed out, "what changed was the language (increasingly stripped down) and the communicative element (increasingly more open). Yet there were not great modifications in its experimental zeal, and much less in its persistant intention to arrive at the point." The emphasis was, undoubtedly, "on *communicating*, on getting to the reader, on including him."[6] It was a poetry that went against the current, transgressed the established social and cultural order, challenged the individualism intrinsic to modernity and the neo-colonial condition. A poetry that renounced authoritarian monologue, the usurption of the other's voice, and accepted without fanaticism the values and language of the people on the streets. A critical and auto-critical poetry that ultimately defied oppressive social realities as much as redeeming revolutionary ideals.[7]

For Saúl Yurkievich, poets like Juan Gelman—and the Ecuadorian Jorge Enrique Adoum, the Cuban Fayad Jamís, the Mexican Juan Bañuelos, the Venezuelan Juan Calzadilla, the Salvadoran Roque Dalton, among others—want "to ally a progressive ideology with a formal breadth." At the same time "formalists" and "realists," they propose to insert their writing "in contemporary reality [...] as a process of material production, and not as a [...] transcendental trampoline, an aphrodisiac or hallucinogen." Thus, "[w]ithout dogmas, asymmetries or censure," they want "to say the totality of what can be said without alienating the specific requirements of the poetic sign, knowing it to be above all verbal instance subject to its own processes," which they strive to exploit and develop. They practice "a polyvalent, polyphonic, plurivocal poetic" that seeks "to unite political and artistic advances."[8] With *The Poems of Sidney West*, Spanish American revolutionary poetry has become a dialogic discourse. The use of narrativity permits the creation of a web of voices, greater participatory democracy in artistic representation.

The Poems of Sidney West belongs to both Juan Gelman's cycle of "translations" and his narrative poems. The shift toward narrativity has been, according to Pedro Lastra, one of the characteristics of Spanish American poetry produced between the end of the 1950s and the beginning of the 1970s. Other characteristics that Lastra draws attention to in this poetry, which could also be called "neo-avant-garde," are "the appearance of the character, mask or double in poetic space;" "intertextuality as recourse;" and "reflection on literature within literature."[9] Opting for "intertextuality as recourse" is related to the rise of the narrative in a stricter sense, the poorly named "boom of the Latin American novel," lead by García Márquez and other authors, and it is a topic that remains to be studied.[10] Then again, narrativity does not lead to the development of epic poetry. On the contrary, surpassing once more a traditional Western opposition, the result is a discourse that continues to serve lyricism.

The contents of The Poems of Sidney West pose a radical question: must human beings in modern society—and moreover, in a peripheral enclave like Argentina—die in order to recuperate their human condition? Yet such denial, according to the dialectic-materialist world view that Juan Gelman's work is based on, proves ultimately to be a negation of the negation. Symbolically, death is at first the refutation of the social condition of these thirty-five oppressed and repressed characters. Yet with this death does not come transcendence, access to a world outside of action and knowledge, or the existential return to nothing, where humans lose all agency. Something happens after the passing of these characters, their absence causes unforeseen consequences, generates certain kinds of presence. From an individual perspective, transformation equals death, yet this does not mean, at a social and natural level, the end, but another beginning. The transformation of these characters is not only inevitable; it is moreover a socially positive, fecund, beneficial process.

The Poems of Sidney West opens with a verse that, without a shadow of a doubt, refers to the kingdom of the marvelous: "it began to rain cows." This unusual phenomenon, like many others that occur throughout the book, is not registered or accepted as natural by Western logos, what is generally referred to as science. By opting for magic as part of popular culture, for the marvelous not as invention but part of reality, the poetic subject challenges imperialist reason. In order to decolonize representation—and the very referent, a society marked by a colonial past and a neo-colonial present—a singular approach to magic realism is produced. The term is pertinent for it underscores that "the rational, linear world of Western realist fiction is placed against alter/native narrative modes that expose the hidden and naturalized cultural formation on which Western narratives are based."[11]

The Poems of Sidney West offers us only one clue about when these accounts take place, yet it is significant: chester carmichael "dead in the fall of 1962." The space is even more precise and determined, always within the real or imagined United States. This territorial emplacement, beyond Argentina's borders, constitutes a frank questioning by Juan Gelman of the nationalism and populism on the rise during the era. According to this decolonizing political gesture, what is being challenged is not only individualist romanticism but also the collectivist realism promoted by Stalinism and deferred to with its variants by Latin American coreligionists. Ultimately, both this romanticism and realism are based on a voluntarist and thus idealist conception of social movement, which produces a distorted representation of reality. What is sought here is the destruction of the self, a redefinition of the poetic I that, like these stories' characters, experiences a metamorphosis, de/composes to achieve the com/position of the subordinated other.

From the margins of modernity, without renouncing his condition as enemy poet—Dalton believed that "whatever his quality, his stature, his finesse, his creative capacity, his success, the poet can only be to the bourgeoisie: servant, clown or enemy"[12]—Juan Gelman has created a work that is made up of an impressive corpus in quantity and quality. A work that reaffirms the capability of poetry to apprehend, in its historicity, a contradictory character and diversity, natural and social phenomena. As Julio Cortázar warned in 1981, the reality of these poems "is exactly and literally the reality of horror, the death and hope of modern-day Argentina."[13] The foundation of this poetic is to conceive writing, without lessening its essential condition of creative practice, as an instrument not only to interpret but to transform the world. And what is offered is a model of a poet conscious of his relationship to nature and society, who truly unites art and life, revolutionary ideology and aesthetic revolution.

The use of translation as a tool for poetic creation that distinguishes Juan Gelman's work, reaches its apex with *The Poems of Sidney West*. María del Carmen Sillato has stressed how this device, along with heteronomy and intertextuality, is "an expression of alterity by recognizing the other-author, the other-text, and the other-language as co-participants in the elaboration of a textual universe."[14] As for us, we only have left to mention that these translations of Gelman's translation have been carried out under the most rigorous accuracy. It is this, upon conveying the poetic subject's message, which makes beautiful expression possible. There is much in these texts that is truly untranslatable, just as surely there was in the imaginary American's originals. Something must have gotten lost in the translation, and something must have remained, for the whole maintains its power, humanity, lucidity. In sum, we hope this translation is not treason but, on the contrary, an act of fidelity.

KATHERINE HEDEEN and VÍCTOR RODRÍGUEZ NÚÑEZ
Gambier, March 8, 2005–May 24, 2006

Notes

1 Cited in Jorge Boccanera, *Confiar en el misterio: Viaje por la poesía de Juan Gelman* (Buenos Aires: Sudamericana, 1994) 25.

2 Among others, *El juego en que andamos* (1959), *Velorio del solo* (1961), *Gotán* (1962), *Cólera buey* (1965), *Fábulas* (1971), *Hechos y relaciones* (1980), *Si dulcemente* (1980), *Citas y comentarios* (1982), *Hacia el sur* (1982), *Exilio* (in collaboration with Osvaldo Bayer, 1984, *La junta luz* (1985), *Com/posiciones* (1986), *Interrupciones II* (1986), *Interrupciones I* (1988), *Anunciaciones* (1988), *Carta a mi madre* (1989), *Salarios del impío* (1993), *Dibaxu* (1994), and *Incompletamente* (1997).

3 Mario Benedetti, *Los poetas comunicantes*, 2nd. ed. (Mexico: Marcha Editores, 1981) 187.

4 These are Gelman's principal anthologies: *Poesía* (Havana, 1968), *Obra poética* (Buenos Aires, 1975), *Poesía* (Havana, 1985), *La abierta oscuridad* (Mexico, 1993), *Antología poética* (Montevideo, 1994), *De palabra* (Madrid, 1994), *Antología poética: 1956–1994* (Buenos Aires, 1994), *En el hoy y mañana y ayer: Antología personal* (Mexico, 2000), and *Pesar todo: Antología* (Mexico, 2001).

5 Juan Gelman, *Unthinkable Tenderness: Selected Poems*, ed. and trans. Joan Lindgren, intro. Eduardo Galeano (Berkeley: U of California P, 1997).

6 Benedetti 15–16.

7 According to Mike Gonzalez y David Treece, "'conversational poetry'— though the concept of a democratic poetry seems preferable—locates the collective at the heart of poetic language. This means recuperating the traditions of popular culture, the patterns and rhythms of speech, the alternative history told in the oral myth, and molding the redemptive revolutionary vision out of the material of everyday life. The process is not reductive, but expansive." *The Gathering of Voices: The Twentieth-Century Poetry of Latin American* (London: Verso, 1992) 305.

8 Saúl Yurkievich, *La confabulación con la palabra* (Madrid: Taurus, 1978) 153.

9 Pedro Lastra, "Notas sobre la poesía hispanoamericana actual", *Inti* 18–19 (1983–84): ix–xvii.

10 An excellent collection of critical essays on Gelman is Lilián Uribe, ed., *Como temblor del aire: La poesía de Juan Gelman* (Montevideo: Vintén, 1995).

11 Bill Ashcroft, Gareth Griffiths and Helen Tiffin, *Key Concepts in Post-Colonial Studies* (New York: Routledge, 1998) 133.

12 Roque Dalton continued: "The clown is an 'independent' servant who manages nothing better than the limits of his own 'liberty' and who one day will confront the people with the argument that the bourgeoisie 'really has sensitivity'. He who is really a servant can wear the uniform of lackey or minister or cultural representative abroad, including silk pajamas for entering the bed of the most distinguished lady. The enemy poet is above all else the enemy poet. He who claims his wages not in flattery or dollars but in persecutions, prisons, bullets. And not only does he lack a uniform or tails or suit, but every day he ends up with fewer things until the only thing he has is a pair of patched shirts but clean as unparalleled poetry." *Poemas clandestinos/Clandestine Poems*, ed. Barbara Paschke and Eric Weaver, trad. Jack Hirschmen, intro. Margaret Randall (Willimantic: Curbstone P, 1986) 2.

13 Julio Cortázar, "Contra las telarañas de la costumbre", *De palabra*, by Juan Gelman (Madrid: Visor, 1994) 5–8.

14 María del Carmen Sillato, *Juan Gelman: Las estrategias de la otredad: Heteronimia, intertextualidad, traducción* (Rosario: Beatriz Viterbo, 1996) 17.

La traducción, ¿ es traición?
La poesía, ¿es traducción?

— Po I-po

Translation, is it treason?
Poetry, is it translation?

— Po I-po

lamento por la muerte de parsifal hoolig

empezó a llover vacas
y en vista de la situación reinante en el país
los estudiantes de agronomía sembraron desconcierto
los profesores de ingeniería proclamaron su virginidad
los bedeles de la filosofía aceitaron las grampas de la razón
      intelectual
los maestros de matemáticas verificaron llorando el dos más dos
los alumnos de lenguaje inventaron buenas malas palabras

esto ocurrió mientras al mismo tiempo
un oleaje de nostalgia invadía las camas del país
y las parejas entre sí se miraban como desconocidos
y el crepúsculo era servido en el almuerzo por padres y madres
y el dolor o la pena iba vistiendo lentamente a los chiquitines
y a unos se les caía el pecho y la espalda a otros y nada a
      los demás
y a Dios lo encontraron muerto varias veces
y los viejos volaban por el aire agarrados a sus testículos resecos
y las viejas lanzaban exclamaciones y sentían puntadas en
      la memoria o el olvido según
y varios perros asentían y brindaban con armenio coñac
y a un hombre lo encontraron muerto varias veces

junto a un viernes de carnaval arrancado del carnaval
bajo una invasión de insultos otoñales
o sobre elefantes azules parados en la mejilla de Mr. Hollow
o alrededor de alondras en dulce desafío vocal con el verano
encontraron muerto a ese hombre
con las manos abiertamente grises
las caderas desordenadas por los sucesos de Chicago
un resto de viento en la garganta
25 centavos de dólar en el bolsillo y su águila quieta
con las plumas mojadas por la lluvia infernal

lament for the death of parsifal hoolig

it began to rain cows
and in light of the prevailing situation in the country
the agronomy students sowed disorder
the engineering professors proclaimed their virginity
the philosophy janitors oiled the staples of intellectual reason
the math teachers verified crying the two plus two
the language learners invented good bad words

while this was happening
a wave of nostalgia invaded the country's beds
and the couples look at each other as strangers
and twilight was served for lunch by mothers and fathers
and the pain or the hurt slowly dressed the little ones
and the chests fell off some and the backs off others and to the
    rest nothing fell off at all
and they found God dead several times
and old men flew through the air holding tightly to their dried
    testicles
and old women hurled exclamations and felt painful stitches
    in their memory or oblivion
and various dogs approved and toasted with Armenian cognac
and they found a man dead several times

near a carnival Friday ripped from the carnival
under an invasion of autumnal insults
or over blue elephants standing on Mr. Hollow's cheek
or close by the larks in sweet vocal challenge with summer
they found that man dead
with his hands openly gray
his hips disordered by the events in Chicago
remains of wind in his throat
25 cents in his pocket and its still eagle
with feathers wet from infernal rain

¡ah queridos!
¡esa lluvia llovió años y años sobre el pavimento de Hereby Street
sin borrar la más mínima huella de lo acontecido!
¡sin mojar ninguna de las humillaciones ni uno solo de los miedos
de ese hombre con las caderas revueltas tiradas en la calle
tarde para que sus terrores puedan mezclarse con el agua y
      pudrirse y terminar!

así murió parsifal hoolig
cerró los ojos silenciosos
conservó la costumbre de no protestar
fue un difunto valiente
y aunque no tuvo necrológica en el *New York Times* ni el *Chicago*
      Tribune se ocupó de él
no se quejó cuando lo recogieron en un camión del servicio
      municipal
a él y a su aspecto melancólico

y si alguno supone que esto es triste
si alguno va a pararse a decir que esto es triste
sepa que esto es exactamente lo que pasó
que ninguna otra cosa pasó sino esto
bajo este cielo o bóveda celeste

oh dear ones!
that rain fell years and years on the pavement of Hereby Street
without ever erasing the slightest trace of what had happened!
without dampening one of the humiliations not even one of the fears
of that man with hips scrambled tossed in the street
late so his terrors can mix with water and rot and end!

and so died parsifal hoolig
he closed his silent eyes
kept the custom of not protesting
was a brave dead man
and while his obituary did not appear in the *New York Times* and the
      Chicago Tribune paid no attention to him
he did not complain when they picked him up in a truck from the city
him and his melancholy look

and if someone supposes this is sad
if someone is going to stand up and say it is sad
know this is exactly what happened
nothing else happened but this
under this sky or vault of heaven

lamento por el arbolito de philip

philip se sacó la camisa servil
llena de tardes de oficina y sonrisas al jefe
y asesinatos de su niño románticamente hablando
su niño operado cortado transplantado injertado
de bucólicas primaveras y Ginger Street volando alto verdadera
en la tarde de agosto cruel o gris

se quedó en pecho philip y cuando
se quedó en pecho hizo el recuento feliz de cuando:
le sacó la lengua al maestro (a espaldas del maestro)
le hizo la higa a la patria potestad (a espaldas de la patria potestad)
formó cuernitos con la mano contra toda invasión maternal (a
        espaldas de toda invasión maternal)

se burló del ejército la iglesia (a espaldas del ejército la iglesia)
en general de cuando
ejerció su rebelde corazón (dentro de lo posible)
fortificó sus entretelas acostumbradas al vuelo (siempre que el tiempo
        lo permita)
engañó a su mujer (con permiso)

philip era glorioso esas noches de whisky y hasta vino
exóticamente consumido con referencias a la costa del sol
una palabra encantadora lo detenía semanas y semanas a su alrededor
sol por ejemplo
o sol digamos
o la palabra sol
como si philip buscara lejos de la sociedad industrial
fuentes de luz fuentes de sombras fuentes

qué coraje hablar del sol

lament for philip's tiny tree

philip removed his servile shirt
filled with afternoons in the office and smiles to the boss
and assassinations of his child romantically speaking
his child operated cut transplanted grafted
of bucolic springs and Ginger Street flying high true
in the cruel or gray August afternoon

philip remained shirtless and when
he remained shirtless he happily recounted when:
he stuck his tongue out at the teacher (behind teacher's back)
gave the finger to paternal authority (behind paternal authority's back)
cuckolded all kind of maternal invasion (behind maternal invasion's back)

mocked the army the church (behind army's church's back)
in general of when
he exercised his rebellious heart (as much as he could)
fortified his interlinings accustomed to flight (always as time allowed)
cheated on his wife (with her permission)

philip was glorious those nights filled with whiskey and even wine
exotically consumed with references to the costa del sol
an enchanted word close by would detain him for weeks and weeks
sun for example
or sun let's say
or the word sun
as if philip searched for far from industrial society
fountains of light fountains of shadow fountains

what courage to speak of the sun

como suele ocurrir philip murió
una tarde lenta amarilla buena callada en los tejados
no hablaremos de cómo lo lloró su mujer (a sus espaldas)
o el ejército la iglesia (a sus espaldas)
o el mundo en particular y en general súbitamente de espaldas:
su viuda le plantó un arbolito sobre la tumba en Cincinnati
que creció bendecido por los jugos del cielo
y también se curvó

y si alguien piensa que lo triste es la vida de philip
fíjese en el arbolito le ruego
fíjese en el arbolito por favor

hay varias formas de ser mejor dicho
muchas formas de ser:
llamarse Hughes
hablar arameo mojarlo con té
estallar contra la tristeza del mundo
pero a ustedes les pido que se fijen
en el curvado arbolito
tiernamente inclinado sobre philip
su pecho en pena en piel como se dice

ni un pajarito nunca
cantó o lloró sobre ese árbol
verde y todo inclinado
inclinado

as it often happens philip died
a slow yellowing good quiet afternoon on the roofs
we will not speak of how his wife cried (behind his back)
or the army or the church (behind his back)
or the world in particular and in general suddenly
with its back turned:
his widow planted a tiny tree near his tomb in Cincinnati
that grew blessed by the sky's juices
and also curved

and if anyone thinks of how sad philip's life was
I beg them think of the tiny tree
think of the tiny tree please

there are various ways to be better said
many ways of being
to call oneself Hughes
speak Aramaic wet it with tea
explode against the sadness in the world
but I ask each of you to look closely at
the curved tiny tree
tenderly leaning over philip
his chest in pain in skin as they say

not even once a small bird
has sung or cried in that tree
green and leaning
leaning

lamento por gallagher bentham

cuando gallagher bentham murió
se produjo un curioso fenómeno:
a las vecinas les creció el odio como si hubiera aumentado la
      papa
feroces y rapaces comenzaron a insultar su memoria
como si el deber obligación o tarea de gallagher bentham
fuera ser inmortal

siendo que él se preocupaba cuidadosamente
de vivir imperfecto a fin de no irritar a los dioses
jamás se cuidó de ser bueno sin ganas
pecó y gozó como los mil diablos
que sin duda lo habitaban de noche
y lo obligaban a escribir versos sacrílegos
en perjuicio de su alma

así
creció famoso por su desparpajo y sus caricias
"ahí va gallagher bentham el desgraciado malparido" decían
      las vecinas a sus hijos
y lo mostraban con el dedo
pero de noche soñaban con él
de noche una extraña nube o mano o seda
se les metía en la garganta soñando con él

¡ah gallagher bentham gran padre!
pueblos enteros habría fundado nada más con sus hijos
de haberlos querido tener
de no haber sido por los versos
que no piden de comer y es de lo poco que tienen a favor

de modo que murió nomás y la gente
desconcertada por la falta de ejemplo del mal ejemplo
o con la sensación de haber perdido algo de su libertad

lament for gallagher bentham

when gallagher bentham died
it produced a curious phenomena:
the neighbor women's hate for him grew as if the price of potatoes
    had risen
ferocious and rapacious they began to insult his memory
as if the duty obligation or assignment of gallagher bentham
was to be immortal

being he worried carefully
of living imperfectly as to not irritate the gods
never once concerned himself with being good without wanting to be
he sinned and enjoyed it as a thousand devils
who undoubtedly inhabited him each night
and obliged him to write sacrilegious verse
to damage his soul

so
he became famous for his nerve and his caresses
"there goes gallagher bentham that wretched son of a bitch" said
the neighbor women to their children
and they pointed at him
but at night they dreamt of him
at night a strange cloud or hand or silk
entered their throats dreaming of him

oh gallagher bentham great father!
entire towns he would have founded with nothing more than his
    children
had he wanted to have them
had if not been for the verses
who do not ask to eat and it is the little in their favor

and so it happened he just up and died and the people
disconcerted by the lack of example of bad example
or with the sensation they had lost something of their liberty

designó representantes que entrevistaron a gallagher bentham
y por más preguntas que le hicieron
sólo escucharon el ruido de abejas en su cuerpo
como si estuviera haciendo miel
o más versos en otra cosa siempre

es difícil saber por qué el vecindario de Spoker Hill llegó a
        odiarlo así
lo descuartizaron una mañana de otoño para alegría de los
        chicos
no hubo más nubes en garganta de mujer
ni desquites feroces en la cama con marido extrañado
o hasta sueños de las más delicadas que llenaban la noche
y hacían girar al viento y llover

todos los arbolitos de Spoker Hill se secaron
menos el tábano real que volaba y volaba
alrededor de gallagher bentham o sus últimas mieles

designated representatives who interviewed gallagher bentham
and no matter the number of questions they asked
they heard only the sound of bees in his body
as if honey were being made
or more verses he always into something else

it is difficult to know why the Spoker Hill neighborhood came to
      hate him so
one autumn morning they chopped him up to the happiness of the
      children
there were no more clouds in wives' throats
no ferocious retaliations in bed with astonished husbands
not even dreams of the most delicate kind that filled the night
and made it rain and the wind stir

all the tiny trees of Spoker Hill dried up
all except the royal horsefly who buzzed round and round
gallagher bentham or his last sweetnesses

lamento por la tórtola de butch butchanam

el pobre butch butchanam pasó sus años últimos
cuidando a una tórtola ciega y sin querer ver a nadie
en solidaridad con el pájaro al que amaba y cuidaba
y a veces aleteaba en su hombro dejando caer
un dulce sonido a naranjos azules girando por el cielo
a demonios de pie sobre un ratón
a monos de piedra sorprendidos en el acto de hacer

"oh tórtola" decía butch butchanam "amas la ceguera
y yo convertí mi corazón en ceguera
para que vueles alrededor de él y te quedes"
pero lo que debe desaparecer
todo lo que se masca come chupa bebe o saborea
venía con el crepúsculo y tristeza para butch
tristeza para butch

el cual:
soñaba con el desierto sembrado de calaveras de vaca
los castillos de arena instantánea o polvo rápidamente quieto en
        tierra
los oleajes (como de serpiente) del tiempo en Melody Spring
y los antepasados que ya no conocían el dolor ni el dolor de la muerte
y hablaban un idioma lento amarillo feliz
como un lazo de oro en el cuello

noches y noches soñó butch butchanam
hasta que supo que iba a morir
enfiló su cama hacia el sur y se acostó de espaldas al cielo
y dejó escrito en la tórtola que lo enterraran de espaldas al cielo
y aquí yace de espaldas al cielo mirando todo lo que baja y sube
en Melody pueblo de miserables que:

lament for butch butchanam's turtle-dove

poor butch butchanam spent his last years
caring for a blind turtle-dove and refused to see anyone
in solidarity with the bird he loved and cared for
and sometimes it would flutter wings upon his shoulder letting fall
a sweet sound as blue orange trees spinning through the sky
as demons standing on a mouse
as stone monkeys surprised in the act of making

"oh turtle-dove" butch butchanam would say "you love blindness
and I have changed my heart to blindness
so you will fly close by and stay"
but what ought to disappear
everything one chews eats sucks drinks or tastes
would come with the twilight and sadness for butch
sadness for butch

who:
dreamt of the desert scattered with cow skulls
instantaneous sand castles or rapidly still dust over earth
waves (as those of a serpent) of time in Melody Spring
and ancestors who now knew no pain nor the pain of death
and spoke a language slow yellow happy
as a golden noose around one's neck

night after night butch butchanam dreamt
until he knew he was to die
he pointed his bed towards the south and lied down with his back to
        the sky
and left written on the turtle-dove to bury him with his back to the
        sky
and here he lies with his back to the sky watching all that goes down
        and up
in Melody wretched town that:

degollaron la tórtola la asaron la comieron
y comprobaron con cristiano horror
que los miraba desde el plato
con el recuerdo de sus ojos

slit the turtle-dove's throat roasted it ate it
and proved with Christian horror
that it looked up at them from the plate
with the memory of its eyes

lamento por el pájaro de chester carmichael

todas las niñas cantan en Melody Spring
todos los niños bailan en Melody Spring
y las ancianas tejen los ancianos fuman sus pipas de espuma de
      mar en Melody Spring
menos chester carmichael muerto en el otoño de 1962

previamente se había deshojado como un árbol
plumas vientos pedazos de memoria se le fueron cayendo
lo último fue una mujer o lo que quedaba de una mujer
semirroída masticada seca y aún fosforescente
que iluminó a chester carmichael noches y noches
y no se apagó todavía y brilla donde empieza el camino del sur

él está oscuro:
no tanto por eso de la tierra y la muerte
el tiempo le trabajó la cara como un angelito
y ahora está desnudo de alternativas decadencias furias
entre suaves raíces y demás compañeros de estación

se acabó chester carmichael
se fue con un nardo en la mano acompañado por cien mil monos
que cantaban bailaban como las niñas y los niños
de Melody Spring
no hubo sollozos gritos flores sobre su corazón
sólo un pájaro bello que lo miraba fijo
y ahora vigila su cabeza

¡ah pajarito!
cada tanto se inclina sobre chester carmichael y oye lo que está
      devolviendo
tranquilo como el sol

lament for chester carmichael's bird

all the young girls sing in Melody Spring
all the young boys dance in Melody Spring
and the old women knit the old men smoke their sea foam pipes
      in Melody Spring
all except chester carmichael dead in the fall of 1962

previously he had lost his leaves as a tree
feathers winds pieces of memory falling all around him
the last to fall was a woman or what was left of a woman
semi-gnawed chewed dry and even phosphorescent
who illuminated chester carmichael night after night
and still could not be extinguished and shines where the southern
      road begins

he is dark:
not so much because of earth and death
time reworked his face as a small angel
and now he is naked without alternatives decadences furies
among smooth roots and the rest of his seasonal companions

chester carmichael was finished
he left with a spikenard in his hand accompanied by one hundred
      thousand monkeys
who danced and sang as the young girls and boys of Melody Spring
there were no sobs screams flowers over his heart
only a beautiful bird who would stare at him
and now watches over his head

oh tiny bird!
every so often it bends over chester carmichael and hears what he
      is giving back
calm as the sun

lamento por el sapo de stanley hook

stanley hook llegó a Melody Spring un jueves de noche con un sapo
     en la mano
"oh sapo" le decía "sapito mío íntimo mortal y moral y coral
no preocupado por esta finitud
no sacudido por triste condición furiosa" le decía

"oh caballito cantor de la humedad oh pedazo esmeralda"
le decía stanley hook al sapo que llevaba en la mano
y todos comprendieron que él amaba al sapo que llevaba en la mano
más allá de accidentes geográficos sociológicos demográficos
     climáticos
más allá de cualquiera condición

"oye mío" decía "hay muerte y vida día y noche sombra y luz"
decía stanley hook "y sin embargo te amo sapo
como amaba a las rosas tempranas esa mujer de Lesbos
pero más y tu olor es más bello porque te puedo oler"

decía stanley hook y se tocaba la garganta
como raspándose el crepúsculo que entraba y avanzaba y le ponía el
     pecho gris
gris la memoria feo el corazón
"oye sapo" decía mostrándole el suelo
"los parientes de abajo también están divididos ni siquiera se
     hablan"
decía stanley hook "qué bárbara tristeza" decía ante el asombro
     popular
los brillos del silencio popular
que se ponía como un sol

lament for stanley hook's toad

stanley hook arrived in Melody Spring one Thursday night with a toad
     in his hand
"oh toad" he would say "my tiny toad intimate mortal and moral and
     coral
unworried by this finiteness
not shaken by sad furious condition" he would say

"oh tiny horse bard of humidity oh bit of emerald"
stanley hook would say to the toad he carried in his hand
and all understood he loved that toad he carried in his hand
above and beyond geographical sociological demographic climatic
     accidents
above and beyond what ever kind of condition

"listen my tiny one" he would say "there is death and life day and
     night shadow and light"
stanley hook would say "and nevertheless I love you toad
as that woman from Lesbos loved early roses
but more and your scent is even more beautiful because I can smell
     you"

stanley hook would say and he would touch his throat
as to scratch the twilight that would enter and advance and turn his
     chest gray
gray his memory ugly his heart
"listen toad" he would say showing him the floor
"the relatives below are divided as well they do not even speak to each
     other"
stanley hook would say "what barbaric sadness" he would say to
     popular astonishment
the gleams of popular silence
would set as a sun

esa noche naturalmente stanley hook se murió
antes dio terribles puñetazos a las paredes de su cuarto en
     representación de sí mismo
mientras el sapo sólo el sapo todo el sapo
seguía con el jueves

todo esto es verdad:
hay quien vive como si fuera inmortal
otros se cuidan como si valieran la pena
y el sapo de stanley hook se quedó solo

that night naturally stanley hook died
beforehand he punched terribly at the walls of his room in
     representation of himself
while the toad only the toad the entire toad continued on with
     Thursday

all of this is true:
there are those who live as if they were immortal
others who care for themselves as if they mattered
and stanley hook's toad remained alone

lamento por los ojos de vernon vries

todas las palomas de la tarde perseguían a vernon vries y era maravilloso
verlo huir de tanta crueldad o blancor
pero él creía hacer esfuerzos para volar con ellas
y en realidad hacía esfuerzos para volar con ellas pobrecitas

"¡oh vernon! verdadero de arriba verdadero de abajo poco hay en el
      mundo"
decía al escapar o volar y sus ojos manchados por la dura contemplación
no vivían en paz perpetuamente hechos y deshechos
vivían mal o tristes o encontrando pobreza

se supo que los ojos de vernon vries vivían así:
adorando pájaros ríos cataratas el océano extenso
las lluvias los calores las amadas que giran por el aire
esos ojos se encerraban a veces en el baño para llorar
"ah" decían "si árboles fuéramos"

pero eso se supo después
las palomas reventaron los ojos de vernon vries una tarde
y vieron las raíces que bajaban a tierra
y también las comieron gozosas por todo lo que vuela

hay palomas que brillan al sol
cuando piensan en vernon vries como hojitas les salen del pico
pero a él se lo llevaron los tábanos
y estaba como rojo de miel

fue de ver los aplausos que hubieron
cuando los ojos de vernon vries se alejaron
como fuegos sin ruido apagándose
en fantástico vuelo orbital

lament for vernon vries' eyes

all the afternoon's doves would chase vernon vries and it was wonderful
to see him running from so much cruelty or whiteness
but he believed he made the effort to fly with them
and actually he was making the effort to fly with them poor things

"oh vernon! true from above and below very little there is in this world"
he would say upon escaping or flying and his eyes stained from such
        harsh contemplation
did not live in peace perpetually made or unmade
they lived poorly or sad or finding poverty

it was soon known vernon vries' eyes lived in this way:
adoring birds rivers waterfalls extensive ocean
rains heats beloved women who spun through the air
those eyes would often lock themselves in the bathroom to cry
"oh" they would say "if only trees we were"

but this was known after
doves poked out vernon vries' eyes one afternoon
and they saw the roots sinking to earth
and ate them enjoying for all that flies

there are doves who shine in the sun
when they think of vernon vries it is as if bits of leaf fall from their
        beaks
but horseflies carried him away
and he was as if red from honey

what a sight to see the applause there was
when vernon vries' eyes grew distant
as soundless fires being extinguished
in fantastic orbital flight

lamento por el ciruelo de cab cunningham

cab cunningham tenía cincuenta años y un ciruelo
cuando descubrió la maldad
los ojos se le pusieron verdes la boca gris y azul alternativamente
daba como señales al empezar el día

eso no es todo:
del vientre le empezaron a subir vientos que lo hacían volar
y girar alrededor del planeta y de su casa
como un alma maldita o en pena que trabajara a todo tren

¡oh! cab cunningham no se hacía ninguna ilusión
con lágrimas secas regaba el ciruelo
que florecía de espaldas al asunto
peleando con los pájaros que lo venían a romper

eso daba una música que cab cunningham escuchaba a la tarde a
          modo de consuelo
entre ciruelo y pájaros había una especie de tratado o misión
y prolongaban temblores ruidos
miedos luchas elecciones furias

"¡oh cab!" solía decir cab
"he aquí que las casualidades que organizan tu cuerpo
son como los monos santos de Panini
caprichosos y verdaderos tristes"

decía cab cunningham y más
"oh carbono y nitrógeno detenidos por mí" decía
"¿oro serán ahora que termine? ¿adónde irán ustedes huesos
o carne sangre ojo perfil dientes que era?"

lament for cab cunningham's plum tree

cab cunningham was fifty years old and had a plum tree
when he discovered evil
his eyes turned green his mouth gray and blue alternatively
he sent up what seemed signals upon beginning each day

that is not all:
from his insides came winds forcing him to fly
and circle the planet and his house
as a soul cursed or in pain working at full speed

oh! cab cunningham had no illusions
with dry tears he watered the plum tree
that bloomed with its back to the matter
arguing with the birds who would come to break its branches

this created a music cab cunningham would listen to in the afternoons
        as a way of consolation
between the plum tree and the birds there was a kind of treaty or
        mission
and tremors noises fears struggles
choices furies prolonged

"oh cab!" cab would often say
"I have here the accidents organizing your body
are as the sainted monkeys of Panini
capricious and truly sad"

cab cunningham would say and more
"oh carbon and nitrogen retained by me" he would say
"will you be gold when you finish? where will you go bones
or flesh blood eye profile teeth that I was?"

nunca se supo adónde fueron o
qué fue de la congoja de cab cunningham los viernes por la tarde
cuando era hermoso y parecía encenderse
bajo el cielo imparcial

pero se supo lo siguiente:
toda la biología atada por cab cunningham
crepitó libre cuando él murió
y áhi el ciruelo se detuvo
nunca más trabajó con los pájaros
nunca más hizo ruido, ciruelito

it was never known where they went or
what happened to cab cunningham's anguish those Friday afternoons
when he was handsome and seemed to ignite
under the impartial sky

but this was known:
all biology bundled up by cab cunningham
crackled free when he died
and there the plum tree lingered
never again worked with birds
never again made noise, you, tiny plum tree

lamento por los que envidiaron a david cassidy

sap sap deibi coli pik decía david cassidy a los pies
de su melancolía en primavera ¡oh!
esa melancolía sonaba como siete cañones grandes de la
        primera guerra mundial
cuando él la agitaba o bailaba con su hermoso costado

pero ahora callar
david cassidy sube por las calles del pueblo
y es como si subiera un oleaje seco frío
más negro que la cólera que ardió

con todo eso ¿qué hacer? ¿eh presidentes?
se le evaporaron jugos entrañas humedades a david cassidy
dejándole huesos tirantes
crepitaciones cuando roza el otoño

¿alguno sabe realmente qué hacer?
david cassidy pisa rosas muertas ha mucho
y levanta un olor a podrido frágil
como la tía francesa que se escapó al amanecer

qué pies señor algún día
david cassidy se encontrará varado en Cochrane Street o en la
        esquina del cine
y no habrá más remedio que regarlo y cuidarlo del sol

david cassidy seguirá convirtiéndose en rosas distraídas que los
        niños arrancarán
será un bello final una bella continuación mejor dicho
en vez de andar vagando por tanta tierra agua fuego y otoño
como todo lo que se tuesta asa quema o chamusca

lament for those who envied david cassidy

sap sap deibi coli pic david cassidy would say at the feet
of his melancholy in springtime oh!
that melancholy sounded off like seven huge cannons from World War I
when he would shake it or dance with its beautiful side

but now to be quiet
david cassidy walks up the streets of town
and it is as if a cold dry wave were rising
blacker than burning anger

with all this what to do? huh presidents?
david cassidy's juices insides humidities evaporated
leaving his bones strained
crackling when autumn brushes by

does anyone really know what to do?
for some time david cassidy steps on roses dead long ago
and raises a scent of rot fragile
like the French aunt who escaped at dawn

what feet mister one day
david cassidy will find himself beached on Cochrane Street or on the
        movie house's corner
and there will be no other choice than to water him and protect him
        from sunlight

david cassidy will continue to change into distracted roses that children
        will pick
it will be a beautiful ending a beautiful continuation better said
instead of wandering through so much earth water fire and autumn
as all that is toasted roasted burned or scorched

y los que lo envidiaron se morirán de rabia o rabiosos
no irán a pájaros ni a peces ni nada
mientras que david cassidy
cantará todo lo que tenga que cantar

and those who envied him will die from anger or angry
they will not go to birds or fish or anything at all
while david cassidy
will sing all that he has to sing

lamento por el día español de raf maloney

entre las cosas que raf maloney tenía
había una dinámica de la penetración orgánica y moral
una fisiología de la continuidad del cuerpo
una ética de la sensibilidad nerviosa

ninguna de la cual le servía para nada
se lo veía oscurecer día tras día
mirando al este en estado de inocencia
sin llorar eso sí raf maloney no llora

había una melancolía también grande gorda marrón
y sobre todo un pájaro raf maloney
cuidaba a un pájaro de cuello largo frío
en una pared de su casa

"pájaro" le decía al pájaro "¿te crece el cuello para ver
los pensamientos que te suben del corazón?" le decía
raf maloney
"¿para palparlos mucho y medirlos?" le decía
pero el pájaro callaba completamente

raf maloney tenía también
un día español ancho abierto con olor a merluza
fresco glorioso alto
lo había plantado en el fondo detrás del perejil

allí se acostaba a ver el cielo cuando todo llovía
y había sol para él y vino y tabaco portugués
"¿ves esta furia en paz pájaro?" le decía al pájaro
"¿la ve tu cuello pájaro?" decía raf maloney

cuando raf maloney murió lo cortaron al pájaro
y comprobaron que daba cielo como sol
cielo no como noche
como sol

lament for raf maloney's spanish day

among the things raf maloney had
there was a dynamic of organic and moral penetration
a physiology of the body's continuity
an ethic of nervous sensibility

none of which served for anything
you could see him darken day after day
looking eastward in a state of innocence
without crying one thing is certain raf maloney does not cry

there was a melancholy also large fat brown
and above all a bird raf maloney
cared for a long and cold-necked bird
on a wall of his house

"bird" he would say to the bird "does your neck grow so you can see
thoughts rising from your heart?" raf maloney would say
"to grope and measure them?" he would say
but the bird kept completely silent

raf maloney also had
a Spanish day wide open that smelled like hake
fresh glorious tall
he had planted it in the back behind the parsley

there he would lie down to see the sky when everything rained
and there was sun for him and wine and Portuguese tobacco
"do you see this fury at peace bird?" he would say to the bird
"does your neck see it bird?" raf maloney would say

when raf maloney died they sliced up his bird
and they proved it shed sky as sun
sky not as night
as sun

el cuello lo tenía noche
y daba cielo como sol
así era el pájaro de raf maloney
que se murió cualquiera de estos días

his neck was night
and shed sky as sun
such was raf maloney's bird
who died one of these days

lamento por el uteró de mecha vaugham

mecha vaugham vivió la mayor parte en su uteró
lejos de otros ruidos del mundo o mundanales
y conoció paisajes raros llenos de pájaros nerviosos
y conoció paisajes

"oh bichos" decía mecha vaugham dirigiéndose a los bichos
que poblaban su cuerpo y mucho más su sueño
aleteando picoteándole el alma
"oh bichos que me despiertan la voz"

decía mecha vaugham callándose de pronto o intentando volar
"¿qué es esto que me pega al piso?" decía
zangoloteando chapoteando
con gran horror o fastidio de los vecinos del 3

"pies que piesan en vez de alar o cómo/
sería el mundo el buey lo que se hija/
si no nos devoráramos/
si amorásemos mucho" decía mecha vaugham

"si fuéramos o fuésemos/ como rostros humanos/
empezando de a dos/
completos en el resto" decía mecha derrumbándose
finalmente en el suelo

un día pasó lo que sigue:
pájaro de voz tenor que la amoraba mucho
antes de ser devorado del todo
plantó un arbolito en su alma

lament for mecha vaugham's uterus

mecha vaugham lived much of the time in her uterus
far from other mundane or worldly noises
and discovered strange landscapes filled with nervous birds
and she discovered landscapes

"oh bugs" mecha vaugham would say directing herself to the bugs
that populated her body and even more so her sleep
fluttering pecking at her soul
"oh bugs that awaken my voice"

mecha vaugham would say suddenly silent or intending to fly
"what is it that keeps me stuck to the ground?" she would say
fidgeting splashing
to the great horror or annoyance of the neighbors who lived in
        number 3

"feet that grow feet instead of wings or how/
would be the world ox what is childed/
if we did not devour each other
if we loveloved so much" mecha vaugham would say

"if we were or we were/as human faces/
beginning two by two
complete in the rest" mecha would say collapsing
finally to the ground

one day this happened:
bird with tenor voice who loveloved her very much
before being completely devoured
planted a tiny tree in her soul

mecha vaugham devoró a pájaro pero
el arbolito creció creció
empezó a cantarle de noche
el tenorino

no la dejó dormir
no la dejó vivir y cuando mecha vaugham murió
salió otra vez volando del árbol
el pájaro ese pájaro

a mecha vaugham le alfombraron la tumba
con pedacitos dulces de su mismo uteró
todos los pájaros del mundo al atardecer picoteaban allí o aleteaban
todos del mundo menos uno

mecha vaugham devoured the bird but
the tiny tree grew and grew
the tiny tenor
began to sing to her at night

it would not let her sleep
it would not let her live and when mecha vaugham died
the bird that bird
left again taking flight from the tree

they carpeted mecha vaugham's tomb
with sweet tiny pieces of her very uterus
all of the world's birds in the evening would peck there or flutter
all of the world's birds but one

lamento por la nuca de tom steward

el día que tom steward alzó vuelo montado en su furia
fue realmente memorable:
el sol no se detuvo la tierra no dejó de girar
la máquina celeste siguió trabajando

pero él volaba él
dejaba atrás países continentes
con las manos mojadas de viento
¡oh tom steward!

¡oh tom y steward volador!
tomó la lira y empezó a cantar entre nubes
o ángeles y demonios de Dios atraídos
por los vapores negros que le salían de la boca

"caballos" cantaba "caballos depravacos
cerebelentes áspimos taquerres" cantaba tom steward
y en sólo un arco de volar quemaba
camísculas herpentes

¡qué páramos con un hombre solito había en su voz!
tom steward se detuvo en el aire vio su nuca
y dio vueltas y vueltas aterrizando al fin
en el revés de sus días y vio:

a un hombre que volaba
al sol salir a la tierra girar
la máquina celeste trabajar
a tom steward convertido en tom steward y triste

no voló nunca más en su vida pero
no le pudieron arrancar
el pedazo de viento entre las piernas
lleno de guerras cábalas eneros

[42]

lament for tom steward's nape

the day tom steward took flight mounted on his fury
was truly memorable:
the sun did not linger the world did not stop spinning
the celestial machine continued its work

but he flew he
left behind countries continents
with his hands wet from wind
oh tom steward!

oh tom and steward flyer!
he brought his lyre and began to sing among the clouds
or God's angels and demons attracted
by the black vapors that would leak from his mouth

"horses" he would sing "depraved horses
cerebelentes áspimos taquerres" tom steward would sing
and in only one arc of flight he would burn
camísculas herpentes

what wastelands with a lonely man there was in his voice
tom steward stopped in mid air saw his nape
and spun round and round landing finally
on the other side of his days and he saw:

a man who flew
the sun come out the world turn
the celestial machine at work
tom steward changed to tom steward and sad

he never again in his life flew but
they could never rip out
the piece of wind between his legs
filled with wars cabalas Januarys

a media hora de enterrarlo en consecuencia
salió volando del cementerio de Oak
hizo un arco en el cielo furioso sobre el silencio vecinal
en el lugar de su tumba no hay flores
crecen silbidos caballos crecen

within a half an hour of burying consequently
he left Oak's cemetery flying
making an arc in the furious sky over the neighborhood silence
there are no flowers at his tomb
whistles grow horses grow

lamento por los alelíes de ost maloney

cuando ost maloney en Carville Louisiana vio el mar
se revisó la mala memoria de sus días
como árbol verde lento
que sacudieron hacia el sur

encontró:
piedra negra sobre mañanas en Dakota cuando era libre sobre
      la tierra y el sol
piedra negra sobre madre acostada dulce bajo la tierra y el sol
piedra negra sobre piedra negra y no blanca

así
ost maloney decidió beberse el mar todo
para que nada fuese otra cosa
que Dakota devorada por la mañana suave

¡oh madre acostada sobre maloney como pedazos de alelí!
ost perfumaba todo el mar de la siesta y el ciclón de sus tardes
le cerraba la boca
le cerraba la boca en realidad

pocas veces hubo más valiente comboi en Carville:
enlazó al sol para alumbrarse
se tomó el mar como un whisky
guardó a su madre vivamuerta sin paz

claro que eso le comió la sombra
y donde come uno comen dos
ost que pacía en el Atlántico
maloney con las velas mezcladas en el viento

todos los marineros quieren al compañero
todos los marineros saben que ost maloney
sudó caballos como quien
abre los brazos para el mar

lament for ost maloney's wallflowers

when ost maloney in Carville Louisiana saw the sea
he examined the poor memory of his days
as tree green slow
that was shaken towards the south

he found:
black stone over mornings in Dakota when he was free on the earth
    and sun
black stone over mother lying sweet beneath the earth and sun
black stone over black stone and not white

so
ost maloney decided to drink the entire sea
so nothing could be anything else
but Dakota devoured by the gentle morning

oh mother lying on maloney as pieces of wallflower!
ost perfumed the entire siesta sea and his afternoon's cyclone
closed his mouth
closed his mouth actually

very few times had there been a more valuable cowboy in Carville:
he lassoed the sun to light himself up
drank the sea as a shot of whiskey
kept his alivedead mother without peace

of course this ate up his shadow
and where one eats two eat
ost who grazed in the Atlantic
maloney with his sails mixed in wind

all the sailors love that fellow
all the sailors know ost maloney
sweat horses as someone who
opens his arms to the sea

no fue en yerba que se convirtió maloney en perla o en coral
sino en cosa con mucho mal olor
que ojalá metan en la tierra algún día
ojalá teja la sombra podrida del aéreo alelí

"quiero ser bello" repetía ost maloney mirándose caer
mientras un brillo le subía
de la boca o valor
para los sucesores

maloney did not change to grass or pearl or coral
but something that stunk
hopefully one day they put it in the ground
hopefully it weaves the rotten shadow of aerial wallflower

"I want to be beautiful" ost maloney would repeat watching himself fall
while a brightness rose
from his mouth or bravery
for his successors

lamento por las aguas de bigart sample

¡oh bigart sample desgarrado en el monte!
ya no se oye su palpitar
se lo comieron los mosquitos las moscas
esas malarias sudamericanas

de su boca mezclada a la tierra sube
cada tanto un insulto padre
como crepitaciones en la noche
seca dura podrida

¿adónde fue bigart sample ahora?
¿adónde está en este minuto
que el cielo vira solo sin sol?
nadie sabe qué es de bigart sample ahora

la tierra le tapó las manos
la tierra se lo tragó
como evitándole vergüenzas
el poco amor universal

nadie sabe si le dan de comer a bigart sample
nadie sabe si le dan de beber
si lo crían en un botellón verde
si va a brotar a fin de año

por el barranco donde tienen su guarida los loros
pasa en forma de río que no llegaba al mar
lleno de peces de oro
bigart sample

no puede abrir la boca sin que empiece a llover
por eso está callado
no puede abrir la boca bigart sample
por eso calla calla

lament for bigart sample's waters

oh bigart sample torn on the mountain!
now no one hears his throbs
he has been eaten by mosquitoes flies
those South American malarias

from his mouth mixed with earth rises
every so often an insult father
as cracklings in the
dry hard rotten night

where did bigart sample go now?
where is he in this minute
that the sky twists alone without sun?
no one knows what is bigart sample's now

the land covered his hands
the land swallowed him up
as avoiding shame
the little there is of universal love

no one knows if they feed bigart sample
no one knows if they give him to drink
if they raise him in a large green bottle
if he will bud at year's end

in the ravine where the parrots have their cave
he passes in the form of a river that never arrived to sea
filled with golden fish
bigart sample

he cannot open his mouth without it beginning to rain
so he keeps quiet
he cannot open his mouth bigart sample
so he keeps quiet quiet

lamento por los pies de andrew sinclair

cuando en Toledo Ohio andrew sinclair
empezó a caminar sobre el mundo
dijo "esto es así" y no lloró
pensó lo verde de la época

acostó la cabeza en los pechos maternos como fatigado de
        pronto por tanta comprobación
los pechos daban flores de leche que caían al piso
y calentaban la memoria
ahora que andrew sinclair es grande

andrew sinclair es grande o es triste
con las candelas encendidas pasó lo bajo de la noche
¡oh corazón ardiente hecho pedazos!
los fue sembrando como fieras o furias

¿pero andrew sinclair está aquí?
¿todavía hace sonar su tristeza como un terrible cañón?
¿no caza pajaritos?
¿anda por áhi andrew sinclair?

en la mitad de su memoria la mamá está de pie
dándole de comer a las gallinas o lavando los platos
con manos lentas bellas grises
que daban brillo como el sol

y abrigaban al andrew sinclair ¡ah caminante!
los demonios del valle le comieron los pies
pero él se inclinaba bajo el sol
brillando como madre

lament for andrew sinclair's feet

when in Toledo Ohio andrew sinclair
began to walk on the world
he said "this is the way it is" and did not cry
he thought in the green of the era

he laid his head down on maternal breasts as if suddenly fatigued
        by so much verification
the breasts bloomed flowers of milk that would fall to the floor
and would warm his memory
now that andrew sinclair is grown

andrew sinclair is grown or sad
with the fires burning he spent the worst of the night
oh burning heart broken to pieces!
he went about sowing them as fiends or furies

but is andrew sinclair here?
does he still sound his sadness as a terrible cannon?
does he not hunt small birds?
is andrew sinclair still here?

in one half of his memory his mother stands
feeding the chickens or washing dishes
with slow beautiful gray hands
that shone as the sun

they warmly clothed andrew sinclair ah traveller
the valley's demons feasted on his feet
but he leaned beneath the sun
shining as mother

los demonios tienen dos cuernos en la cabeza y pelos en los pies
y echan llamas por la boca y el culo
se comen los ratones sin pelar
bailan como gitanos se beben de un trago medio balde de agua

pero andrew sinclair no
él tiene un joven corazón
lleno de islas con tigres y garzas
bellísimo bellísimo

abajo de andrew sinclair había un río
y más abajo un sol
y debajo la noche
para nosotros dos

the demons are two-horned and have hair on their feet
blow fire from their mouth and ass
eat unskinned rats
dance as gypsies drink half a pail of water in one swallow

but not andrew sinclair
he has a young heart
filled with islands of tigers and herons
so beautiful so beautiful

below andrew sinclair there was a river
and further below a sun
and beneath the night
for the both of us

lamento por las flores de david burnham

flores de miel flores de piel flores
calientes salían de david burnham
quieto en el aire frío lunar
sin remedio sin adioses sin Dios

¡ah david burnham!
su clavícula clavada en el cosmos era la que más florecía
extrañas vidas daba para la época
en que la gente era infeliz

y preguntaba ¿cómo era el niño david en la clase de inglés?
nunca se supo cómo era
pero está quieto entre fulgores
su cabeza se la come la luz

david burnham amó este final
no quiso a la tierra ni al agua
como cantaba al disolverse
inclinado hacia el sol

que le tapó las manos los ojos los pies
cuidándolo como a palomo ciego
en tanto cae la noche padre y madre
como oso silencioso

las cuatro caras del dolor se apagaron
para david burnham navegando o ardiendo todavía
dulce dulce
detrás del espectáculo

así terminó david burnham se le caía un polvo fino
como jazmín donde avanza la noche
aplasta y se perfuma
¡ah solo en el espacio!

lament for david burnham's flowers

flowers of honey flowers of skin flowers
hot they grew from david burnham
still in the cold lunar air
without fail without good-byes without God

ah david burnham!
his collarbone nailed to the cosmos flowered more than any other
bloomed strange lives for the era
when people were unhappy

and it asked how did young david do in English class?
it was never known
but he is still in the resplendence
his head feasts on the light

david burnham loved this ending
he did not love the land or water
as he sang upon dissolving
leaning towards the sun

that covered his hands eyes feet
caring for him as a blind pigeon
so the night fell father and mother
as silent bear

the four faces of pain were extinguished
for david burnham navigating or burning still
sweet sweet
behind the spectacle

so david burnham ended a fine dust fell over him
as jasmine where the night advances
crushes and perfumes
ah alone in space!

lamento por el vuelo de bob chambers

la vez que a bob chambers lo vieron estaba
poniendo lento el día
dura la vista claro el corazón
le dieron una cama de rosas que fue a tirar al mar

entonces
del costado se le alzaban como especie de oleajes
carnes que se soñaban alas a bob chambers y no pasaron de su piel
en esta edad de tanta carestía

¡ah caramba!
¡ah bob ah chambers dos en su vehículo terrestre!
olvidados yacen ahora bajo sus capas de volar quedándose
y tanta pena apenas se soporta

pero qué hacer
bob esperaba al viento sur
"madre vieja tengo en casa" decía
y chambers vivía vuelto al norte con la mesa puesta

nunca se pusieron de acuerdo sobre este punto cardinal
así ocurrió lo que se supo:
tirando a un lado y a otro lado bob chambers se rompió
la soledad o perros se comieron su agujero central

todo el pueblo lo vio
a bob partir a chambers estallar en la mañana lenta
nunca hubo espectáculo igual y todos aplaudieron
y todos aplaudieron

menos la amiga que lloraba por bob
el que dejó el amor para mañana
menos la amiga que lloraba por chambers
el que dejó el amor para la noche

lament for bob chamber's flight

the one time they saw bob chambers he was
slowing down the day
vision strong heart clear
they gave him a bed of roses that he went to throw to the sea

then
from his side rose as a kind of swell
meats that dreamt themselves wings for bob chambers and did not
        pass through his skin
in this age of so much famine

ah caramba!
ah bob ah chambers two in their terrestrial vehicle
forgotten they lie now under their flying capes remaining
and so much pain is hardly endured

but what to do
bob waited for the southern wind
"my old mother is at home" he would say
and chambers lived returned to the north with the table set

they never came to an agreement about this cardinal point
and so it happened what was later known:
tossing and turning bob chambers broke
his solitude or dogs ate his central hole

the entire town saw him
bob leave chambers burst into the slow morning
never had there been such a spectacle and they all applauded
and they all applauded

all except a girlfriend who cried for bob
he who left love for tomorrow
all except a girlfriend who cried for chambers
he who left love for the night

lavaron a la amiga con rosas y limón
le dejaron los pies en agua fría
y nadie habla de bob chambers
se la pasan desarmándolo tristes como señores

bob chambers no protesta
viajaba por la muerte montado en un burrito
con la mejilla cerca de la luna tan alta
y una almohadita para el sol

they bathed the girlfriend in roses and lime
they left her feet in cold water
and no one speaks of bob chambers
they pass by her disarming him sad as gentlemen

bob chambers does not argue
he traveled through death mounted on a tiny burrow
with his cheek near the so high moon
and a tiny pillow for the sun

lamento por los pies de carmichael o'shaughnessy

carmichael o'shaughnessy mi dios
con el camino en la mano era un planeta
girando y girando en la mañana cerrada
como cubierto de lirios y de trigos

¡ah carmichael!
qué grandes fierros le crecían en los pies
cuando se andaba al gallo primo cantor
y al segundo callado

a carmichael se la caían pedazos
de rabia pura de la cara
que iba dejando como árboles
que crecieron como árboles al costado del camino

no pájaros no vientos no señoras
les movían las ramas sino
años de mal amor y desgracia
años en que el amor viene mal

o mal y triste y destrozado como
la margarita que besó el león
a la solombra del atardecer
donde carmichael lloró un poco

por abajo por arriba por la ventanita
que nadie abre iba carmichael
con el camino en la mano como
paquete de dolor

hasta que un día los pies se le pusieron verdes
áhi carmichael paró
ya rojo ya mitad ya parecido
y dulce fue su desventaja

lament for carmichael o'shaughnessy's feet

carmichael o'shaughnessy my god
with road in his hand he was a planet
spinning and spinning in the closed morning
as if covered in lilies and wheat

ah carmichael!
what large pieces of iron grew on his feet
when he would walk as a rooster first cantor
and as the second quiet

pieces of pure rage fell
from carmichael's face
he went about leaving them behind as trees
that grew as trees do along the side of the road

not birds not winds not ladies
could move the branches instead
years of bad love and disgrace
years in which love arrives poorly

or badly and sadly and destroyed as
the daisy who kissed the lion
in the shade of the afternoon
where carmichael cried a bit

up and down past the tiny window
that no one opens went carmichael
with road in his hand like
package of pain

until one day his feet turned green
there carmichael stopped
already red already in half already alike
and sweet was his disadvantage

toda la sombra que cae de carmichael o'shaughnessy
pega en el suelo y se va al sol
pero antes canta como dos pechos de mujer
o sea canta canta

all the shade that falls from carmichael o'shaughnessy
hits ground and then travels to the sun
but before doing so it sings as a woman's two breasts
or rather it sings sings

lamento por la tripa de helen carmody

hombros hermosos brazos hermosos tripa tan linda pie chiquito
pero también marido viejo regalaron a helen carmody
los diablos de Karthum los marcos de oro
tanta sabiduría acumulada

tanta sabiduría ¿no va para la muerte?
¡ah helen! ¡qué hermosos ojos tiene helen!
de allí crecían sus pechos verdaderamente y no de su mujer
los pechos suyos

un día que las notas del buey rey en la mañana clara
entraban y salían de los amores de helen como
pan de vestir a la hora de salir a la puerta
la llamaron para oírla llorar

"no apartes la muerte de ti helen" dijeron
"no quiebres el espejo árbol florido"
le dijeron a helen carmody en función
qué triste era todo eso

mejor hubiera sido callar
las verdes hierbas saben dar amarillo
y helen sola oscura
no sabe nada nada

sino callar y deshacerse como
la voz del padre en mesa puesta
no pregunten por qué criaturitas
ella callaba llaba

como las ánforas del hijo triste
ninguno lo tomó de beber
las gallinas todas vestidas de negro
ponen sus huevos conmovidos

lament for helen carmody's gut

beautiful shoulders beautiful arms gut so pretty small foot
but also old husband were given to helen carmody
Karthum's devils golden frames
so much accumulated wisdom

so much wisdom does it not all go towards death?
ah helen! what beautiful eyes helen has!
from there grew breasts truly and not those of his wife
her own breasts

one day in which the notes of the ox king in the clear
      morning
entered and left helen's loves as
bread dressed up at the time to head for the door
they called to her to hear her cry

"do not leave death behind helen" they said
"do not break the mirror flowering tree"
they told helen carmody in function
how sad this all was

it would have been better to keep quiet
the green grasses know how to bloom yellow
and helen alone dark
knows nothing nothing

but to keep quiet and undo herself as
a father's voice at a set table
do not ask why tiny creatures
she kept quiet quiet

as a sad child's amphoras
no one drank it
the hens all dressed in black
lay their disturbed eggs

pero helen carmody ya no
no la persigan a caballo yeguas
mámenle la memoria
ah siempre para siempre

but now do not
pursue helen carmody on mares
suck her memory
ah always for always

lamento por el pelo de bright morgan

"hop hop alba amo" decía a caballo de Alabama bright morgan
había nacido al lado de donde se quedaron los juntadores de pasto
indios choctaw que leían las nubes
frenadas por el sur los Apalaches tanta desolación

dios mío tanta desolación no alcanzó para un buen río
"no alcanzaste para un buen río mi Dios" decía bright morgan
"ah distraído" decía a caballo entre Sam Dale William Bankhead (que
      tenía cabeza de pájaro señor) y aún la Julia Tutwiler (reformadora
      social consolatriz de presos poetisa)
otros notables del lugar

sí
"¡ah muererío muererío!" decía bright morgan sin parar de correr
pensando en la madre que vio a siete hijos decapitar subida a su tejado
y después se tiró del tejado

bright morgan hablaba también
de las culebras y alacranes que se comieron el corazón amargo
de 7 hermanos 7 camino de Aragón
ola que ola la maripola no pasa nadie nadie

no pasa nadie por el cuerpo de bright morgan ya
más que el viento y la arena volada por el aire
porque se va a morir
lo dejarán salir

lament for bright morgan's hair

"hop hop dawn master" bright morgan would say on horseback from
    Alabama
he had been born on the side where the gatherers of pasture remained
Choctaw Indians who read the clouds stopped by
south Apalaches so much desolation

my god so much desolation was not enough for a good river
"you were not enough for a good river my god" bright morgan would say
"ah absent-minded" he would say on horseback amid Sam Dale William
    Bankhead (who had the head of bird mister) and even Julia Tutwiler
    (social reformer inmate consoler poet)
other notable members of the place

yes
"ah so many dead so many dead!" bright morgan would say continuing
    to run
thinking of a mother who saw her seven children decapitated up on her
    roof
and afterwards she threw herself from the roof

bright morgan would talk too
of snakes and scorpions who ate the bitter heart
of 7 brothers 7 on the road to Aragón
ola que ola maripola no one no one passes by

now no one passes by bright morgan's body
but the winds and sand blown through the air
because he is going to die
they will let him leave

y la madre se subirá al tejado y dirá:
"quien a este hijo pierde merece ser apedreada
le pediría uñas al águila pezuñas a la bestia con pezuñas
y no le dejaría a la tierra ese muchacho lindo no"

decía la madre de bright morgan:
"no dejaría que la tierra lo pudra le deshaga la frente hermosa no
yo se lo arrancaría a la tierra de trigo sembrada
con dolor robaría a la tierra ese hijo tan bueno cara de plata"

decía la madre de bright morgan:
"que se llevó la tierra con golpe rabioso no
ese pequeño novio no alcanzó a criar hijos
dejó casa vacía por casa llena de compañeros sin luz"

mientras tanto bright morgan murió
"no le echen tierra sobre la frente hermosa" pedía la madre pero él
crecía a la derecha y a la izquierda
abajo arriba iba creciendo como una vaca grande

cuando el pelo de bright morgan paró
toda Alabama se detuvo un instante
pero ya no decía "madre madre no me dejes salir"
ola que ola la maripola no pasa nadie nadie

and his mother will climb the roof and say
"she who loses her son deserves to be stoned
she would ask the eagle for its claws the cloven-hoofed beast for its
        hooves
and would not leave that beautiful boy to the land no"

bright morgan's mother said:
"I would not let the land rot him undo his beautiful forehead no
I would pull him from the land of harvested wheat
painfully I would rob the land of that good son silver face"

bright morgan's mother said:
"the land did not carry him with angry blow no
that tiny groom had no time to raise children
he left empty home for one filled with lightless companions"

while she was saying all this bright morgan died
"do not throw dirt on his beautiful forehead" his mother asked but he
grew right and left
down and up he grew as a large cow

when bright morgan's hair stopped
all of Alabama stopped for a moment
but now he did not say "mother mother do not let me go"
ola que ola maripola no one no one passes by

lamento por la camisa de sam dale

sam dale no quería dormir
solo con sus sudores
y a la madre le dijo "madre
búscame novia entre los odios del día"

así creció perseguido por olor
que nunca supo conseguir
la madre madrecía cada noche
pero no había caso

"ah" decía sam dale al final de su chaleco
hermoso como un secretario general
"novia mía ¿por qué no venís?
novia mía ¿qué suelo ató tus sienes?"

la novia de sam dale dormía y hacía amanecer
de sus dos pies salía el sol la luz
y era bella como los pies de Dios
atados siempre siempre

a tanto dolor atados pero no Dios sino el grande amor
duerme atado a profunda claridad
no lo despierten hijos
que duerma duerma duerma

a menos que le den de comer
él duerme porque no le darían de comer
y duerme hermoso hermoso
como la novia de los yules verdes

como la novia del amor primero
ella está muerta y yo la quiero
pero sam dale ni nada
él pedía a la madre por la esposa del río

lament for sam dale's shirt

sam dale did not want to sleep
alone with his sweats
and said to his mother "mother
find me a bride among the hates of the day"

so he grew pursued by odor
that he never knew how to find
his mother would mother every night
but it was not enough

"ah" sam dale would say at the end of his vest
beautiful like a secretary general
"my bride why do you not come?
my bride what floor has tied your temples?"

sam dale's bride slept and made the sky dawn
from her two feet bloomed sunlight
and was beautiful as God's feet
tied always always

so tied to pain but not God rather the great love
sleeps tied to profound clarity
do not wake it children
let it sleep sleep sleep

unless they feed it
it sleeps because they would not feed it
and it sleeps beautiful beautiful
as the bride of green fiestas

as first love's bride
she is dead and I love her
but sam dale nothing at all
he asked his mother for the river's wife

la esposica estaba en el río vestida de amarillo
haciendo una cama grande con las aguas
cortinas con los pájaros para que entre la mañana cantando
y aun la muerte cantando cuando debiera entrar

pero sam dale vigilaba la puerta y Dios no entra por ahí
así que viuda tora marinera se le murió la camisa
y la enterró ya tarde ya tardísimo
y manzanitas de oro había en las ramas

¡gracias que tiene lo perro!
¡ah muérdanos la cara para despertar!
a sam dale lo pusieron en una copa de vidrio
"¡ah tripa dolorosa!" decía hablando del corazón

la flor de su camisa tapó *o mundo* celéstese sam dale
cuándo despertaremos mi dios
novia dormía hermosa hermosa con un lunar de amor
y un ruiseñor que le cantaba enemigos

sam dale cruzó Alabama como un fuego
dejó en herencia una mañana que las gallinas picotearon
y del costado le caían señoras
acabaditas de nacer

¡ah sam dale te tomaron el alma en la mitad del arenal!
no debiera dormir mal ahora a las tres de la tarde tu entierro pasó
al pie de tu retrato ella se arrodilló
pobre con una cuna blanca sola

tiny bride was in the river dressed in yellow
making a large bed with the waters
curtains with birds so the morning enters singing
and even death singing when it should have entered

but sam dale would guard the door and God does not enter there
and so widowed brave sailor his shirt died
and he buried it so late so very late
and tiny golden apples grew from its branches

grace that has the dog!
ah bite our faces to wake us up!
they put sam dale in a glass cup
"ah painful gut" he would say speaking of his heart

the flower of his shirt covered *o mundo* turn sky blue sam dale
when will we wake up my god
bride slept beautiful beautiful with a birthmark of love
and a nightingale that would sing enemies

sam dale crossed Alabama as wild fire
he left as a heritage a morning the hens pecked
and from his side fell ladies
very recently born

ah sam dale they took your soul in the middle of a sandy ground
he should not sleep so poorly at three in the afternoon your funeral
        procession passed
at the foot of your portrait she knelt
poor with a white cradle alone

lamento por la historia de cab calloway

hay hombres con una historia o dos
pero cab calloway tenía otra historia
a nadie la podía mostrar y le pesaba
más que el Día de la Santa Consolación

¡ah cab calloway hijo!
toda sabiduría es poca eso se sabe
con los brazos hundidos hasta el codo en la espesa marea
se le volvían dulces las mujeres

y terribles como un cuento de hadas
la Bella Durmiente se la pasaba despertando
cómo salir del bosque oscuro
cómo salir preguntaba cab calloway

"por áhi anda el cansancio haciendo ruidos" decía pero no
cab calloway arregló su corazón como una casa
puso la mesa y bebió
a la salud de todos los vívientes

ninguno conocía a cab calloway
pero una especie de humo o voz o calor o luz
se les caía en la cabeza según
cuando cab calloway brindaba

de modo que está bien
el pajarito está contento
salta y salta en la jaula y canta
¡ah cab calloway padre!

un día de estos se murió y lo enterraron con sus pies
que asistieron respetuosos a toda la ceremonia
y después se fueron por el campo
y en la pieza de cab calloway lloraban las mujeres

lament for cab calloway's story

there are men with a story or two
but cab calloway had another story
he could not show it to anyone and it weighed him down
more than the Day of Holy Consolation

ah cab calloway son!
all wisdom is slight this is well known
with his arms sunk to the elbows in thick tide
women became sweet to him

and terrible as a fairy tale
Sleeping Beauty spent her time waking up
how to escape from this dark forest
how to escape cab calloway would ask

"that way tiredness noisily walks" he would say but no
cab calloway fixed his heart as a house
he set the table and drank
to the health of all the living

no one knew cab calloway
but a kind of smoke or voice or heat or light
fell on their heads just
as cab calloway was toasting

in a way that is fine
the tiny bird is happy
it jumps and jumps in its cage and sings
ah cab calloway father!

one of these days he died and they buried him with his feet
who respectfully attended the entire ceremony
and afterwards they left for the country
and in cab calloway's bedroom the women cried

cuando las lágrimas se secaron
el pajarito se las comió
el pajarito está contento
salta y salta en la jaula y canta

una mujer a lo mejor le abrazaba los pies a cab calloway
antes de que se fueran por el campo
hundiéndose hasta el codo en la espesa marea
ya vueltos dulces dulces

when their tears dried
the tiny bird ate them
the tiny bird is happy
it jumps and jumps in its cage and sings

a woman probably hugged cab calloway's feet
before they left for the country
fleeing up to their elbows in thick tide
now turned sweet sweet

lamento por la niña blanca de johnny petsum

johnny petsum lloraba por las tardes
en el w. c. de la Coronation Inc Corp
pero poco lloraba
atento al gran señor de la cadena

el gran señor no era
el capataz o dueño o accionista montado en un burro de fuego
el gran señor era un sonido hosco duro vivo patrón
en la cadena que andaba y andaba

mientras uno ponía el tornillo otro la tuerca y todos
el alma el cuerpo la memoria el horror
de olvidar
el día –no la noche– en que los bellos muchachos servían sus amores

y tres aves chiquitas cantaban
por el amor por el dolor por la ceguera
¡ah johnny petsum! habrá navío que te lleve a dormir
alzó las velas para volver a la ciudad

allí johnny petsum mató
al carcelero del rosal
al que envenena las pechugas de ave
al que ensuciaba boca a boca los aires del río

antes de irse a la muera escribió carta
"¿de qué llorás niña blanca?" decía y es cierto
nunca supo de qué
con la ceguera de johnny petsum hicieron un asado

con su amor y dolor hicieron un asado
la niña blanca lloraba debajo de sus besos no dados justamente
de los que un día nacieron altos brillos
ya tarde johnny oh

lament for johnny petsum's white girl

johnny petsum cried every afternoon
in the w.c. of Coronation Inc Corp
but he did not cry too much
aware of the chain's great boss

the great boss was not
the foreman or owner or stockholder mounted on a fiery donkey
the great boss was a sound sullen hard living chief
on the chain that would run and run

while one placed the bolt the other the nut and everyone
the soul the body the memory the horror
of forgetting
the day—not the night—when the beautiful boys served their loves

and three tiny birds sang
for love and for pain for blindness
ah johnny petsum! a ship will carry you off to sleep
it raised its sails to return to the city

there johnny petsum killed
the rose bush's warden
what poisons bird's breast
what dirtied from mouth to mouth the river's airs

before dying he wrote a letter
"why are you crying white girl?" he would say and it is true
he never knew why
they roasted johnny petsum's blindness

they roasted his love and pain
the white girl cried beneath his unjustly given kisses
kisses that one day were born tall brilliant
too late johnny oh

menos para las aves chiquitas
menos para las aves menos mal
que cantaban cantaban
ya ciegas mucho ciegas

not so for the tiny birds
not so for the birds not so bad
that sang and sang
now blind much blind

lamento por el llanto de sim simmons

una mañana de otoño sim simmons
se levantó sin ojos como caídos en favor de la estación
"pero no importa" dijo
y se alisaba la memoria

"no importa realmente no importa" decía sim simmons
poniéndose árboles vacíos en las cuencas
a los que alimentó con estampidos
gritos olvidos silenciosas partes

nocturnos insectos portadores de muerte
rondaban por los árboles
"no importa" decía sim
desplegando sus tiernas alas

y volando todo alrededor del cielo
"si fuese una nube" decía "si fuese un halcón o catástrofe
lo que me come el corazón" decía
"te apagaste paloma" decía sim simmons sin llorar

"no tengo ojos para llorar" decía "sin embargo debiera"
decía recordando que todo vegetal
agua llanto lluvia o río necesita
para abrigar un tierno nido

así que sim simmons se puso a llorar
los árboles se le volaron
y otra vez tuvo ojos para mirar o ver o sufrir
y llorar sin dar comida a nadie

lament for sim simmon's weeping

one autumn morning sim simmons
woke without eyes as if they had fallen in favor of the season
"but no matter" he said
and smoothed his memory

"no matter no matter at all" sim simmons would say
placing empty trees in eye sockets
trees he fed with stampedes
cries forgetfulness silent parts

nocturnal insects death's bearers
made their rounds through the trees
"no matter" sim would say
spreading his tender wings

and circling the sky
"if I were a cloud" he would say "if I were a falcon or catastrophe
what my heart eats away at" he would say
"you have quenched yourself dove" sim simmons would say without
        weeping

"I have no eyes to cry" he would say "but I should"
he would say remembering everything vegetable
water weeping rain or river needs
a tender nest to guard against the cold

and so sim simmons began to weep
the trees flew all around him
and once again he had eyes to watch or to see or to suffer
and to weep without feeding anyone

"me lo merezco" decía sim simmons tarde
"me lo merezco mucho" decía con los ojos ya secos
duros brillantes como sol
bajo la tierra de Alabama

dos ríos nacieron donde lo enterraron
uno hacia el norte otro hacia el sur
para memoria para olvido
y todo el mundo tuvo agua

pero sim simmons no:
miraba hacia abajo
ya merecido o muerto o triste
sin árboles sin árboles

"I deserve it" sim simmons would say late
"I quite deserve it" he would say with his eyes now dry
hard brilliant as the sun
beneath the Alabama land

two rivers were born where they buried him
one toward the north the other toward the south
for memory for oblivion
and everyone had water

but sim simmons did not:
he looked downward
now deserving or dead or sad
without trees without trees

lamento por las yerbas de jack hammerstein

"salud salud" decía jack hammerstein
se la pasaba saludando a:
todos a todos a todos
aunque lloraran ensuciando el mantel
aunque tuvieran leonas bravas

"afuera negra desventura afuera afuera" decía
entrando a cada casa y espantándola con la mano
como si las desgracias fuesen moscas o mosquitos o insectos
y miel la gente en su esplendor

"afuera muerte grima dolor peste o barbaridá de la tristeza"
decía jack hammerstein limpiando esos polvos
o arrancaba la yerba ya vieja crecida
sobre ternuras sobre zapatitos de seda que no hacen ruido en el amor

así jack hammerstein de color amarillo
como si se pasara las noches entre claveles o alelí
en realidad tenía una amada
que se bañaba en agua clara

en realidad tenía una niña/ que se bañaba en agua fría
y le crecían luces suavidades
"qué lindo pelo tienes" le decía jack hammerstein
"qué linda frente ojos boca pechos tienes" le decía jack hammerstein
"qué lindo pie chiquito río de mármol"

"oh muerte que a todos convidás" dijo jack hammerstein ahí
la amada estaba bella bella
y sobre ella crecía yerba esta vez
dando color olor y sombra

lament for jack hammerstein's grasses

"greetings greetings" jack hammerstein would say
he spent his time greeting:
everyone everyone everyone
even though they cried dirtying the tablecloth
even though they had angry lions

"out black misfortune out out" he would say
entering each house and frightening it with his hand
as if mishaps were flies or mosquitoes or insects
and honey people in their splendor

"out death grimness pain stink or sadness' barbarism"
jack hammerstein would say cleaning those dusts
or he would pull up the grass now old and grown
over tendernesses over tiny silk shoes noiseless in love

so jack hammerstein yellow in color
as if he spent nights among carnations or wallflower
actually had a beloved
who bathed in clear water

actually he had a girl/who bathed in cold water
and smoothnesses lights grew from her
"what nice hair you have" jack hammerstein would say to her
"what nice forehead eyes mouth breasts you have" jack
          hammerstein would say
"what a pretty little foot river of marble"

"oh death you who invites everyone" jack hammerstein said there
the beloved was lovely lovely
and this time grass grew over her
giving heat scent and shade

al pie se acostó jack hammerstein para mirarla subir
"afuera desventura afuera afuera" decía y la espantaba con la mano
"afuera muerte grima dolor peste o barbaridá de la tristeza" decía
a los traidores bichos negros que le comían corazón

"salud salud" decía jack hammerstein
no lo pudrió la pena ni la furia
se la pasaba saludando a todos y aún arrancándoles la yerba
pero a su amada no o la miraba subir
desde la mesma muerte

at her feet jack hammerstein would lie down to watch her rise
"out misfortune out out" he would say and frighten it with his hand
"out death grimness pain stink or sadness' barbarism" he would say
to the traitors black bugs eating at his heart

"greetings greetings" jack hammerstein would say
neither pain nor anger rotted him
he spent his time greeting everyone and still pulling the grass from them
but not from his beloved or he would watch her rise
from death itself

lamento por la gente de raf salinger

cuando raf salinger se enamoró o quiso de verdad
salió de sí como de un calabozo
brilló con propia luz
no tuvo tacha ni defecto ni mengua

como caballos como vacas al fin de la jornada
raf salinger vertía sus aguas en plena soledad
fulguró afuera como sol
no pálido de cárcel no en guerra

"cuidado que me lastimás" decía raf salinger
a los hombres de manos ásperas
que como niños están cubiertos de miel
pero le quitan la victoria al vencedor

"oh ángel que te inclinas en la primera mitad"
decía raf salinger furioso cavando
el viento que le envolvía la trasluz
o el revés de los días malos que le comían la verdad

"si el coraje consiste en ser prudente" decía raf salinger
"si los vestidos significan desnudez y miseria
dicha el llanto y cadáver curación te arde amor el odio" decía
con gran perdones finalmente

todas las ventanitas se cerraron
cuando raf salinger murió
una calor le creció entre amor y afuera
juntándole los dos al solito

"ah tiempos no distancias que hay entre mí
entre mi calor y mi sol" decía raf salinger
casi disuelto ya bajo la sombra
que le apagaba el hubo que vivir

lament for raf salinger's people

when raf salinger fell in love or really tried to
he escaped from himself as from a prison cell
he shone with his own light
had no flaw no defect no decay

like horses like cows at the end of the day
raf salinger emptied his waters in complete solitude
he flashed outside like sun
not pale from prison not at war

"be careful you are hurting me" raf salinger would say
to the rough handed men
who as children are covered in honey
but they take away the victory from the victor

"oh angel leaning on the first half"
raf salinger said furiously digging
the wind enveloping the translucence
or the other side of bad days that ate his truth

"if courage consists of being prudent" raf salinger would say
"if dresses mean nakedness and misery happiness weeping
        and cadaver healing
love burns your hate" he would say
finally with great pardons

all the small windows closed
when raf salinger died
a heat grew between love and outside
the two joining the lonely man

"ah times not distances there are between me
between my heat and sun" raf salinger would say
almost dissolved now under the shade
that extinguished the need to live

sobre su gente subió el frecuente olvido
pero raf salinger viajaba abrigado
por un cuerpo desnudo
encontrado o joven

over his people rose frequent oblivion
but raf salinger traveled protected
by a naked body
found or young

lamento por la mano de arthur donovan

cuando arthur donovan vino del sur
hizo una parva con sus maldades resentimientos tristezas
les prendió fuego en el crepúsculo
para espantar a los mosquitos de paso

quedó solísimo apoyado en bellezas
"y qué va a hacer" decía arthur donovan con luz
o suavidad o dulzura pechonas
contando su poquito

"y qué va a hacer" decía
pero una mirada que le dieron como amparo o amor le sostenía el
      esqueleto
en esa mirada arthur donovan estaba parado
y hacía señales contra el mundo

"ah mirada" decía arthur donovan el entendido en sombras
"solo estamos por aquí" decía y ya la noche le rebajaba el sufrimiento
a pájaros a tierra
mojada respirando

cuando arthur donovan murió
sacó una mano afuera extendiéndola
como quien pide lluvia o nido o no tanta soledá
olvido si no hay caso

cómo llovió sobre esa mano
no hubo gente que no llorara por allí
pero ni hojita le creció al puro hueso
comido por el aire

lament for arthur donovan's hand

when arthur donovan came from the south
he made a pile of his badnesses resentments sadnesses
lit them on fire at twilight
to frighten the mosquitoes flying by

he remained so very alone backed in beauties
"and what are you going to do" arthur donovan would say with light
or softness or sweetness large breasted women
counting their tiny bit

"and what are you going to do" he would say
but a glance they gave him like refuge or love preserved his frame
in that glance arthur donovan stood
and signaled against the world

"ah glance" arthur donovan the understood in shadows would say
"we are alone here" he would say and night had lessened his suffering
to birds to earth
wet breathing

when arthur donovan died
he raised his hand extending it
as someone asking for rain or nest or not so much solitude
even oblivion

how it rained over that hand
there wasn't anyone who did not cry there
but not one tiny leaf grew from the pure bone
eaten by air

"y qué va a hacer" decía arthur donovan
mientras el viento lo limpiaba
y él levantaba su mirada famosa
como calor desobediente a la suerte fatal

"and what are you going to do" arthur donovan would say
while the wind cleansed him
and he raised his famous glance
as heat disobedient to fatal luck

lamento por la llama de roy joseph gally

"escátame la sepa" roy joseph gally decía
y una calandria o perro o gran trasluz le levantaba el buey tranquilo
le metía la boca en la carona
le daba dura escarrabeca

por eso
cuando la realidá a manera de alquiler
o dueño o claridad en los ojos dél daba
"escátame la sepa" roy joseph gally decía
sabiendo su canción

"no los pedazos que me quisiera devorar" roy joseph gally cantaba
"no la madera el jeme la bichoca parientes míos amadísimos en esto de
        acabar" cantaba
"hermosa es la mi llama" cantaba "veloz y como seda
y buena y de cuello altivo erguido" cantaba

"y reverbera como estrella o calor" cantaba roy joseph gally
"y nada de lo que va a matar
ninguna piedra o luna que pasa o flor que muere
puede dañar sus cabellos de oro" cantaba

"o rebajarla a frío a sombra" roy joseph gally cantaba
besó a la llama o reina contra el sol dejándolo rompido
"ah vida oscura" dijo "a rescatar"
dijo "pronto" tocándola

por eso
cuando roy joseph gally murió
disimulaba el mucho rato en soledad
peste del pecho es la tristeza

lament for roy joseph gally's flame

"escátame the sepa" roy joseph would say
and a calandra lark or dog or great gleam would lift his tranquil ox
stick his mouth in his saddle
give him hard escarrabeca

and so
when reality by way of renting
or owner or clarity in his eyes appeared
"escátame the sepa" roy joseph gally would say
knowing his song

"not the pieces I would like to devour" roy joseph gally sang
"not the wood the jeme the bichoca my dearly loved relatives in this
        that is ending" he sang
"beautiful is this my flame" he sang "fast and silky
and good and made of arrogant and high held neck" he sang

"and it reverberates like star or heat" sang roy joseph gally
"and nothing it will kill
not rock or moon passing by or dying flower
can harm its golden hair" he sang

"or lower it to cold or shade" roy joseph gally sang
he kissed the flame or queen against the sun leaving it broken
"ah dark life" he said "to rescue"
he said "soon" touching it

and so
when roy joseph gally died
he disguised much of the time in solitude
a chest's plague is sadness

"o la calandria o perro de irse" roy joseph gally cantaba
disperso íntimo reseco
"salud llama veloz"
cantaba quedando quieto ya

"either the colandra lark or dog of departing" roy joseph gally sang
disperse intimate dried
"greetings fast flame"
he sang now remaining still

lamento por el furor de roy hennigan

"¿cómo serán los japoneses?" preguntaba roy hennigan
"¿dónde andarán? ¿por qué cielos? ¿cómo cavan
su marcha hacia el fulgor?" preguntaba acostándose
en las tardes feroces de Ohio

"con tanto ardor calor o fuego eterno" decía
"¿cómo resulta frío este furor? ¿cómo es pedazo nonobstante?"
preguntaba roy hennigan seco
o arrugado a medida de la noche

o encendido de duro en la palor
del mundo en la gran ciega de las últimas
"¿cómo es que pujan mis contrarias?
¿quién las agita o mueve?" preguntaba roy hennigan puro

"¿quién aquí sangra? ¿yo?" decía roy hennigan
"¿quién pega o peca o perra de mi estar?
¿con qué resisten estas partes?"
ya preguntaba en bestia dado

con la mirada recorrió sus llagas
y las llagas mundiales cubrió
apenas pez en claro vivo
¡ah rey roy hennigan a poco!

de su morir estallaron las huelgas
del sertimiento de los pieses mentales
y así roy hennigan calló
y nunca nadie lo lloró

"mejor mejor" decía roy hennigan
"háganme caso niños" decía yéndose
en ala en cúmplase emplumado
pero con luz qué cosa vea

lament for roy hennigan's rage

"What are the Japanese like?" asked roy hennigan
"where might they be? why skies? how do they dig
their march toward brilliance?" he would ask lying down
on Ohio's ferocious afternoons

"with so much heat warmth or eternal fire" he would say
"how can this rage be so cold? how is it pieces nonetheless?"
roy hennigan would ask dry
or wrinkled in proportion to the night

or glowingly tough in the world's pallor
in the last great blind woman
"how is it my adversaries bid?
who shakes or moves them?" roy hennigan asked purely

"who here bleeds? Is it I?" roy hennigan would say
"who hits or sins or dogs my being?
how do these parts resist?"
he now asked in beast given

with his gaze he traversed his wounds
and his worldly wounds barely
covered fish in brilliant clear
ah king roy hennigan at least!

from his dying strikes
of sentiment of mental feets broke out
and so roy hennigan quieted
and no one ever cried for him

"better better" roy hennigan would say
"pay attention children" he would say leaving
on wings on feathered be fulfilled
but with light what might he see

lamento por los idiotas de warren s. w. cormoran

"oh warren warren" gritaban todos los idiotas del pueblo
en la mañana de Santa Mónica sucia
por el hollín los escapes los sueños
rotos o podridos de la noche anterior

qué formidable
extrañas rosas u orquídeas florecían en esa podredumbre caliente
mientras la multitud del bulevar vivaba a warren ese dabliu cormoran
y él se deslizaba de contrabando por el día

"oh warren warren" le decían sobre
la suciedad el mal olor el pésame envolviendo
tanta salud apenas débil
o muda o yendo en dirección a su pérdida

en todo caso era así:
el ser se lo dio la madre en hermoso verdor
a su sombra creció warren como piedra en el río
hasta que la rompió como flecha con suaves ojos disparada

¡y si pudiera olvidar completamente!
"warren warren" gritaba la multitud no dejándolo dormir
o sólo abría su dureza donde
volaba una mosca azul sospechosa

warren ese dabliu cormoran:
¿tenía acaso ají tu sementera?
en todo caso se voló y voló
quiéranlo mucho lagartos

lament for warren s. w. cormoran's idiots

"oh warren warren" all the village idiots yelled
in Santa Monica's morning dirty
from last night's broken or rotten
soot getaways dreams

how formidable
strange roses or orchids bloomed in that hot decay
while the boulevard's multitude cheered warren es double u cormoran
and he slipped on contraband during the day

"oh warren warren" they would say to him above
the dirtiness the foul smell the condolences enveloping
so much health scarcely weak
or mute or going in the direction of its loss

in any case it was like this:
his mother gave him his being in beautiful greenness
in her shadow warren grew as stone in a river
until he broke it like an arrow shot with soft eyes

and if he could only completely forget!
"warren warren" screamed the multitude not letting him sleep
or only opening his hardness where
a suspicious blue fly buzzed

warren es double u cormoran:
did your sowing perhaps reap chili pepper?
in any case he flew and flew
wish him many lizards

denle sombrita en la mitad
tápenlo para el frío
o que lo abrigue la calor
de los sueños podridos de Santa Mónica el hollín
"oh warren warren" gritaban todos los idiotas del pueblo
pero no así por qué así qué pasa con las águilas

give him a bit of shade in the middle
cover him from the cold
or let the heat
of Santa Monica's rotting dreams the soot
warm him
"oh warren warren" all the village idiots yelled
but not that way why that way what happened to the eagles

lamento por las manos de astor frederick

cuando astor frederick murió
plegó alitas y dejó sobre todo sus penas
y un como brillo o resplandor
que lo seguía en el entierro

ni perro ni hombre ni mujer o gato seguía su cajón
por la calle dorada en la mañana del mayo paciente
pero sí el brillo o resplandor
como cantándole cantándole

decía el brillo "astor frederick se va por aquí
al país donde todos se reúnen
sigo las huellas de sus pies besándolas
pero él ya nunca estará solo"

decía el brillo "astor frederick ya nunca más se apenará
de pueblo en pueblo y por alturas su joven corazón
marcará el paso de las lunas
se comerá flores que mueren"

ojala ojala repetían los arcos las piedras podridas de la calle
las pieles de la calle meciéndose por donde
astor frederick sus restos los restos de su dentadura etc
pasaban a gloria mayor

¡ah frederick en la cajita!
lo empaquetaron mucho para siempre
y aunque él no quisiese otra cosa que amor como abrigo o fortín
es como si faltara

la tierra del cementerio de Oak
se lo comió casi por todas
menos las manos eso sí
apoyada la una en la otra

lament for astor frederick's hands

when astor frederick died
he tucked tiny wings and left above all his pain
and like a shine or resplendence
that followed him to the burial

not dog not man not woman or cat followed his coffin
down the golden street on that patient May morning
but the shine or resplendence did
as if singing to him singing to him

the shine would say "astor frederick is passing through here
to the country where everyone meets again
I follow his footsteps kissing them
but now he will never be alone"

the shine would say "astor frederick never again will be troubled
from town to town and on high his young heart
will count off the moon's pace
will eat dying flowers"

hopefully hopefully chanted arches the street's rotten stones
the street's skins swinging wherever
astor frederick his remains the remains of his teeth etc
were passing on to greater glory

ah frederick in the tiny coffin
they packaged him up for always
and even though he wanted nothing but love like a coat or fort
it is as if something were missing

the land at Oak's cemetery
almost ate him entirely up
except his hands that indeed
held on to one another

del silencio que astor frederick hizo
creció una pájara de viento que le volteaba el corazón
menos el brillo o resplandor
cala del mundo mundo mismo

y ésta es la historia de astor frederick ea
ninguna pus paloma o reventón se alzaba nunca de sus nuncas
menos las manos eso sí
apoyada la una en la otra

from the silence astor frederick made
grew a bird of wind that circled his heart
except the shine or resplendence
cutout of the world the world itself

and this is the story of astor frederick yeah
not one pus dove or burst raised itself ever from its nevers
except his hands that indeed
held on to one another

lamento por el sicomoro de tommy derk

a los cuarenta tommy derk descubrió
que él sufría la suerte de su pueblo
que el paraíso a cuenta
lo destinaba a páramo del mundo

¡ah tommy derk cómo lloraba en su entretela o revés!
pero ni así regaba sus tierritas
donde la luz se le apagaba
al pie del sicomoro marrón

y el sicomoro también se apagaba
arrugándolo a tommy derk
cortándole la claridad del pelo
llenándolo de hojas con su nombre muerto escrito allí

¡ah célebres palomas!
ninguna vino a defenderlo a tommy derk
ninguna le dio plumitas para el frío
o pan con leche para el hambre del sur

así que tommy derk se acostó a morir nomás
y pidió que por lo menos lo hacharan
hicieran leña con él algún fuego con él
algún calor o luz o advertencia

cuando lo fueron a encender se le volaron los caballos
se le volaron los caballos a tommy derk
unos fueron al norte otros al frente
unos fueron al tiempo otros a él

pero esa sangre reseca que dejó tommy derk
justísimo debajo de donde ardió
parecía una pluma de pan con leche
con su nombre vivo escrito allí

lament for tommy derk's sycamore

at forty tommy derk discovered
he suffered from the luck of his people
heaven on account of it
destined him to the world's wasteland

ah tommy derk how he cried on his interlining or back!
but not even then did he water his tiny pieces of land
where light turned off
at the foot of his brown sycamore

and the sycamore too turned off
wrinkling tommy derk
cutting the clarity from his hair
filling him with leaves with his dead name written there

ah celebrated doves!
not one came to defend tommy derk
not one gave him tiny feathers for the cold
or bread with milk for his southern hunger

so tommy derk just laid down to die
and asked at least that they hew him
chop him into kindling start a fire with him
some sort of heat or light or warning

when they went to light him his horses flew
tommy derk's horses had flown
some went up north others to the front
some went to time others to him

but that dried blood tommy derk left
in the exact place beneath where he had burned
seemed a feather of bread with milk
with his living name written there

"tommy derk tommy derk" gritaba la plumita
mientras todos los sicomoros de Ohio especialmente
agachaban la cabeza en silencio
como una mala soledad

"tommy derk tommy derk" the tiny feather would scream
while all the sycamores from Ohio especially
bowed their heads in silence
as wretched solitude

lamento por george bentham

alas o páramos o peces
traía la mano de george bentham cálida
de mujer que tocara en plena luna
ya húmeda ya clara ya feliz

¡ah george bentham cómplice!
solía irse solito por los corredores
que atando o uniendo lo tenían a la madre central
la célebre de espumas

la que flotaba cuando empezaba a desnocharse
después de haber amado o ardido la piel se le apagaba
en el fulgor que la sacaba de toda oscuridad
y daba miel y daba leche

y daba george bentham sí señor
una invención total para estos días
negros de pésimas negruras
ah madre a la que hijaron/ como siempre

por eso:
fue cuando Dios comió y bebió
tomó otras medidas populares
que george bentham apareció triste morido

y solo a punto en la mitad del peso
que va de george a bentham y volvía
y quería una llama de oro
brillante y fuerte como el sol

vamos al río a tirar piedras al agua
vamos al río a tirar piedras
vamos a tirar piedras george bentham
nadie te sacará del malagüero

lament for george bentham

wings or wastelands or fish would bring
george bentham's hand warm
from a woman touched in full moon
now wet now clear now happy

ah george bentham accomplice!
he would walk alone through the corridors
that by tying or joining held him to the central mother
the celebrated of foams

she who floated when night began to dress itself
after having loved or burned her skin was extinguished
in the radiance pulling her from all darkness
and offered honey and offered milk

and gave george bentham yes sir
a total invention for these black days
of wretched blacknesses
ah mother the one they childed/as always

and so:
it was when God ate and drank
took other popular measures
that george bentham appeared sad bruised

and alone almost on the half of the weight
that goes from george to bentham and would return
and desired a golden flame
bright and shining as the sun

let's go to the river to throw rocks in the water
let's go to the river to throw rocks
let's go throw rocks george bentham
no one will ever rid you of your bad luck

aunque críes caballos de vientre hermoso
hermoso ampáralos del viento
que cae del propio geroge bentham sí
hoy no te irás te irás mañana

si hoy no te vas te vas mañana
pero no temas a la muerte de ojos de fuego
uno que dice george otro que bentham
y brillan como el sol

quien dice george te habrá cubierto o cubrirá
quien dice bentham también
y nadie sabe cómo hacen
para servirte de comer

allá habrás de crecer george bentham para atrás
en dirección al comienzo de todo
habrá rocío para tu herido corazón
y después bailaremos

por eso:
cuando george bentham murió
por fin callaba la su madre dando
o diciendo suave otra vez
"chaparroncito no me mojes/mío"

even though you raise horses with beautiful beautiful bellies
shelter them from the wind
that falls from george bentham himself yes
today you will not go you will go tomorrow

if you do not go today you go tomorrow
but do not fear the death of fiery eyes
one that says george the other bentham
and shine as the sun

who says george they will have covered you or will cover you
who says bentham too
and no one knows how
they should feed you

there you will grow george bentham from behind
in the direction of where everything begins
there will be dew for your injured heart
and after we will dance

and so:
when george bentham died
his mother finally quieted giving
or softly saying again
"my tiny cloudburst do not drench me/mine"

lamento por la cucharita de sammy mccoy

"en qué consiste el juego de la muerte" preguntó
sammy mccoy parado en sus dos niños
el que fue el que sería
"en qué consiste el juego de la muerte" preguntó sin embargo

antes había bebido toda la leche de la mañana
jugos del cielo o de la vaca madre según
untándola con los sueños que
se le caían de la noche anterior

sammy mccoy era odiado frecuentemente por una mujer
que no le daba hijos sino palos
en la cabeza en el costado
en la mitad del desayuno esa fiebre

de cada palo que le dieron
brotó una flor de leche o fiebre que le comía corazón
pero todo se come el corazón
y sammy nunca se rendía sammy mccoy no se rendía defendiéndose
        con nada:

con la memoria del calor
con la cucharita que perdió una vez revolviendo la infancia
con todo lo que iba rezando o padeciendo
con su pelela mesmamente

así
del pecho le fue una saliendo
una dragona con pañuelo y la luz
como muchacha envuelta en aire

lament for sammy mccoy's tiny spoon

"what is the game of death" sammy mccoy
asked standing on his two children
the one who was the one who would be
"what is the game of death" he asked nonetheless

before he had drank all of the morning's milk
juices of the sky or of a mother cow accordingly
smearing it with the dreams
fallen from him the night before

sammy mccoy was frequently hated by a woman
who did not give him children but blows
to the head to the side
in the middle of breakfast that fever

from each blow they gave him
grew a flower made of milk or a fever that would devour his heart
but everything devours a heart
and sammy never gave up sammy mccoy did not
give up defending himself with nothing:

with the heat's memory
with a tiny spoon that he had lost one time turning over his childhood
with everything he had prayed for or suffered
with his toy doll as well

and so
from his chest emerged
a female dragon with handkerchief and light
as a girl wrapped in air

como dos niños sobre los que niño
sammy mccoy se paraba y
"en qué consiste el juego de la muerte" preguntaba
ya cara a cara de la gran dolora

cuando murió sammy mccoy
los dos niños se le despegaron
el que fue se le pudrió y el que iba a ser también
y de ese modo fueron juntos

lo que la lluvia el sol o gran planeta o la sistema de vivir separan
la muerte lo junta otra vez
pero sammy mccoy habló todavía
"en qué consiste el juego de la muerte" preguntó

y ya más nada preguntó
de sus falanges ángeles con mudos
salían con la boca tapada
a cucharita a memoria o calor

"güeya güeya" gritaban sus dos niños
ninguna mujer salvo la sombra los juntó
qué vergüenza animales
y las caritas les brillaban calientes

así ha de ser caritas de oro
señoras presidentas o almas cuyas acabaran
a los pieses de sammy el que camina
sammy mccoy pisó el sol y partió

as two children over which the child
sammy mccoy stood and
"what is the game of death" he would ask
now face to face with the great pain

when sammy mccoy died
his two children loosened themselves from him
the one who was had rotted and the one who was to be as well
and so they were united

that which the rain the sun or the great planet or life system separates
death brings together once again
but sammy mccoy still spoke
"what is the game of death" he asked

and then he asked nothing more
from their phalanges emerged angels with mutes
their mouths covered
with tiny spoon memory heat

"yah yah" shouted his two children
not one woman except the shade united them
what shame animals
and their tiny faces shone hot

and so it must be tiny golden faces
ladies madam presidents or souls who finished
at the feets of sammy he who walks
sammy mccoy stepped on the sun and left

Fe de erratas

donde dice "salió de sí como de un calabozo" (página tal verso cual)
podría decir "el arbolito creció creció" o alguna otra equivocación
a condición de tener ritmo
ser cierta o verdadera

así escribió sidney west estas líneas que nunca lo amarán
en el frescor de un pozo seco y oscuro
arriba de la tierra deslumbrada por el sol
o solo solo solo

donde dice "si fuéramos o fuésemos/ como rostros humanos"
(página tal verso cual) es como el buey que allí se aró
no podrido por la pena o la furia
disimulando el mucho rato en soledá

¡ah sidney west! aquí terminan (ojalá)
tus repechazos áspimos y pésimos
qué poca por alrededor de este hombre
y adentro qué animal

a sidney west se lo comieron todos los pájaros que supo inventar
la ponina y el nino especialmente
golosos de su estado y pasión
abierta dulce como inútil

donde dice "un día pasó lo que sigue" (página tal verso cual)
había pasado antes la tristeza
y eso es fatal para el poeta
o fue fatal para el peno de west

Errata

where it says "he escaped from himself as from a prison cell" (page
        such and such verse whatever)
it could say "the tiny tree grew and grew" or some other error
as long as it has rhythm
is certain or true

and so sidney west wrote these lines that will never love him
in the freshness of a dry dark well
on top of a world blinded by sun
or alone alone alone

where it says "if we were or we were/as human faces"
(page such and such verse whatever) it is as the ox that ploughed there
not rotted by pain or fury
disguising much of the time in solitude

ah sidney west! here ends (hopefully)
your wretched aspimos leanings
what tiny bit round this man
and what animal within

all those birds that knew how to invent ate sidney west
ponina and nino especially
greedy from their state and passion
open sweet as useless

where it says "one day the following happened" (page such and such
        verse whatever)
sadness had happened by before
and that is fatal for the poet
or it was fatal for west's pain

¡ea bichitos tábanos fulgores que saludaban en el cementerio de Oak!
allí lo pusieron a sidney west que duerma
donde dice "que duerma duerma duerma" (página tal verso cual)
debe decir que duerma y más nada

así que west con el amor primero
fue para sidney marinero
sidney el último en historia
giró con west como burro de noria

que duerma y nada más debe decir (página tal verso cual)
y más nada que duerma y no otra cosa
que duerma duerma duerma
que duerma duerma duerma sidney west

hasta que alen por favor los pieses
que duerma sidney west
hasta que bien nos amoremos
que duerma duerma duerma

el padre lo respire si lo quisiese respirar
acá yacen mezclados como antes
pero que duerma duerma duerma
que duerma sidney west

donde dice "cortinas con los pájaros para que entre la mañana
        cantando" (página tal verso cual)
debe apagarse a la mañana sidney west
que duerma duerma duerma

hey tiny bugs horseflies brilliances greeting in Oak's cemetery!
there they put sidney west let him sleep
where it says "let him sleep sleep sleep" (page such and such verse
    whatever)
it should say let him sleep and nothing more

and so when west with his first love
headed for sidney sailor
sidney the last in history
spun with west as a water wheel's donkey

let him sleep and nothing more should be said (page such and such
    verse whatever)
and nothing more let him sleep and nothing more
let him sleep sleep sleep
let sidney west sleep sleep sleep

until his feets grow wings please
let sidney west sleep
until we love one another well
let him sleep sleep sleep

the father breathes it if he really wants to breath it
here they lie as before
but let him sleep sleep sleep
let sidney west sleep

where it says "curtains with birds so morning enters singing" (page
    such and such verse whatever)
sidney west should turn himself off in the morning
let him sleep sleep sleep